REDEEMED?
SAY SO!

REDEEMED?
SAY SO!

Robert J. Plekker

1817

HARPER & ROW, PUBLISHERS

New York, Hagerstown, San Francisco, London

REDEEMED? SAY SO! Copyright © 1977 by Robert J. Plekker. All rights reserved. Printed in the United States of America. No part of this book may be used or reproduced in any manner whatsoever without written permission except in the case of brief quotations embodied in critical articles and reviews. For information address Harper & Row, Publishers, Inc., 10 East 53rd Street, New York, N.Y. 10022. Published simultaneously in Canada by Fitzhenry & Whiteside Limited, Toronto.

FIRST EDITION

Designed by Eve Callahan

Library of Congress Cataloging in Publication Data

Plekker, Robert J
  Redeemed? Say so!
  1. Witness bearing (Christianity) I. Title.
BV4520.P52   248'.5   76-10004
ISBN 0-06-066652-8

77 78 79 80 10 9 8 7 6 5 4 3 2 1

To my wife
JANE
who encouraged me to study the Scriptures.
And to my mother and father who provided a
Christian home and education to build upon.

"Let the redeemed of the Lord say so, whom he hath redeemed from the hand of the enemy."

PSALM 107:2

Contents

Acknowledgments

I wish to thank all those who helped me during the writing —they know who they are—but especially Mrs. David Bos who pored over each sentence, as only an English teacher could. Dr. Alex DeJong and the Rev. M. S. Jorritsma scrutinized biblical quotes, and Dr. Cliff Christians, with intensive witnessing experience, seminary training, and a Ph.D. in communications, contributed greatly to the final editing.

Foreword

by Pat Boone

"But you will receive power when the Holy Spirit comes on you; and you will be my witnesses."

ACTS 1:8

That verse used to make me uneasy, just a little frightened. I believed in Jesus, had committed my life to Him, been baptized, prayed regularly, led singing at church, lots of good things.

But I didn't feel myself much of a "witness."

When I thought of "witnessing," I thought of street-corner preachers, missionaries in East Africa, folks going door-to-door handing out tracts and inviting people to church. I didn't want to do that, and hoped somehow God wouldn't require it of me.

He didn't, for a long time.

I think He knew I wasn't much of a "witness" anyway. Oh, I could "defend the faith" or expound on a narrow doctrine; I could tell you when, how, and why I'd been baptized; I could point out "humbly" what was wrong with other churches and religions; I would be happy to take you to church with *me*, but would invariably make excuses to keep from wasting my time going with you. I tried to live a good, reasonably religious, balanced life, and was acutely conscious of wanting to please the other members of my church and fulfill their expectations of me. I was only vaguely troubled when I realized our fellowship numbered around three million—and that according to our doctrinal understanding the rest of the world was going to hell! After all, hadn't Jesus said, "small is the gate and narrow the road that leads to life, and only a few find it" (Matt. 7:14)?

My keystone scripture was Phil. 2:12, "work out your own salvation with fear and trembling" (KJV). I was trying to do that—with pretty meager results.

I somehow didn't comprehend, or even see, the next verse —Phil. 2:13—"for it is God who works *in* you to *will* and to *do* what pleases him"!

Sounds like a different ball game, doesn't it?

It sure is.

When you put the two verses together, you see the blueprint of a team effort, a partnership, in which the individual believer does his best from day to day in any and all situations—but the real emphasis is on the action of God Himself to prompt the desire and actually to accomplish His will, in and through that believer!

The trouble with trying to obey only the first verse is that your focus is totally on yourself and your security, with an occasional furtive and fearful glance toward God. The second brings with it a freedom, a release from anxiety and pressure, a sense of destined triumph, of being a pleasing and profitable part of a large Master Plan, whose outlines are too vast and intricate to be seen by the individual but are inevitably Good.

Most of my first thirty-five years was spent working on Phil. 2:12. It was rough, slow going.

But when the thirteenth verse was finally illuminated to me, I became a "witness." It was easy, it was an adventure, it was unavoidable—I can't stop!

And I'm sure that's why Jesus cautioned His closest

friends, His disciples, to "wait . . . you will receive *power* when the Holy Spirit comes on you" (Acts 1:4 and 8).

Power. Holy Spirit. Something supernatural.

Those disciples had been with Jesus three years! They'd seen countless miracles; they'd heard all His lessons and parables; they'd seen Him tried, crucified, and resurrected; they even saw Him ascend into heaven! What "witnesses" they could be! What sermons they could preach!

Why did Jesus want them to wait?

Because He didn't want people just to "witness"; He wanted people to *be* witnesses. He wanted folks who could do more than tell what they believed, to convince others that Jesus was the Messiah; He wanted folks who could *demonstrate* His kind of supernatural life, who would *be* His kind of victorious people.

And that would take power.

That's why He said, in effect, "You've been baptized with water, and that's good. Now in just a few days, I'm going to baptize you with the Holy Spirit. After that happens, you'll have access to a supernatural power that will make you bold and daring, you'll remember and believe what I've taught you, you'll begin to experience a wisdom and compassion that will enable you to move in the face of danger and Satanic opposition—you'll *be* my witnesses" (Acts 1:4–8).

Bob Plekker and I believe that, and have both begun to experience that promise of Jesus. I've seen Bob in action for several years now, and I know him to be a bold witness for our Lord. In this book, Bob shares a lot of common sense and some of his own adventures in witnessing. I really believe you'll be inspired and encouraged by what he shares with you.

I disagree with Bob on one point, though.

He believes that the baptism with the Holy Spirit belongs

to every born again believer, whether they're aware of it or not—that it somehow "happens" at conversion.

I don't.

My study of the Word and my own experience, as I detail in my own book *A New Song*, tell me differently. I was born again and baptized when I was thirteen, and for the next twenty-two years wrestled with Phil. 2:12. It wasn't till I had another *experience*, till I *asked* for and *received* that experience, that I had the power to be a witness, to start experiencing Phil. 2:13.

Jesus said in Luke 11:5-13 that the Father gives the Holy Spirit freely "to those who *ask* him!"—just as He gives salvation to those who ask, who verbalize their faith and their requests (Rom. 10:8-10).

In fact, His promises are virtually unlimited, but they *are* so often conditioned upon asking—Mark 11:24, John 14:13 and 14. Maybe the God who spoke everything into existence wants us to learn the *power that comes with speaking according to His will!*

Just today, reading in John, I was startled to see this from Jesus' own lips: "If you love me, you will do what I command. *I will ask the Father*, and he will give you another Counselor, the Spirit of truth, to be with you forever" (John 14:15, 16, 17a). If God's own Son feels it necessary to ask, concerning the bestowal of the Spirit—I'm extremely hesitant to take Him and His gifts for granted.

That's the way I see it.

But to show you the kind of guy Bob is, even though he sees it differently, he wanted me to write this foreword. He even invited me to explain our different viewpoint here at the outset.

That ought to whet your appetite for his book.

He's a good witness of Jesus' love and saving power and

merciful grace. He knows we're all learning together and that the Holy Spirit is a wonderful teacher.

I think you'll have fun with my brother Bob, and a great life with *our* Big Brother, Jesus.

Beverly Hills, California

Introduction

When I was just a kid, about nine years old, I rode my bike to the beach one day to build the biggest sand castle in the whole world. The project didn't last long; a woman nearby was talking loudly and using God's name in disrespect. I remember being prompted (by the Holy Spirit although I didn't realize He was even working in me) to say something to her about such an outrageous disregard for God. I began to walk over, stopping every couple of steps to see if anyone would catch me. When I stood in front of her, I bent down— eyeball to eyeball—and said (as fast as I could), "God doesn't want you to take His name in vain!" Then I darted away, thrilled that I had probably accomplished God's complete plan for my life right there. After tramping on for at least five minutes, it hit me: I had forgotten my bike! Irksome as it was, I was nonetheless superpleased because I had "witnessed."

A few years later, I laughed at myself for thinking *that* was a witness. Yet, it was, and because it was, I have written this book on witnessing. One of the most difficult aspects of maturing, both physically and spiritually, is learning to identify one's personal potentials and then developing those for Christ without trying to be like someone else.

Christ gave the great Commission to all of us; yet it does not read the same for everyone. All men were not created equal in their abilities to witness for Jesus Christ. This is not grounds for a cop-out on witnessing; rather, it becomes a mandate to amplify the best that we are, to develop fully all our God-given abilities to witness, many of which may yet be hidden.

This book is an effort, therefore, to focus all the power of the Great Commission into one broad picture, with the specific purpose of aiding you to identify with as many aspects of the total witness as God has given you individual and special talents.

A by-product of this approach will be the identification of those areas in which you are not best suited. Not everyone can be the eye, or the ear, or the hand of the body of Christ. By developing an acute awareness of both our abilities and our limitations, we can avoid frustrations often associated with a witness born of an unpolished and unrehearsed sense of duty.

I had every right to be pleased with my witness at age nine. It took all the ability I had at the time. To laugh at myself later for being so awkward and naive indicates that I had not given serious thought to the business of witnessing during those early years.

It wasn't until my years in dental school—when I had opportunity to recognize God's immeasurable wisdom in my human anatomy courses—that I began to spill over verbally about God's marvelous ways once again. The nerves, blood vessels, organs, and connective tissues were in the same exact location in each cadaver that lay on the cold slabs. Because I was talking so much about it, the head of the department came to me one day and said, "Plekker, I understand you are really enjoying this course. [I never enjoyed a course in my life!] Tell me, since you know so much about God, exactly what is the arterial and nerve supply to the soul? Describe its cellular structure for me."

I should have asked him to give me the same description for the mind. (Someday I'd like to write a book entitled "I Should Have Said . . . !") But the school was operated strictly; so I could only say, "Yes, sir, ahhh . . ." and lean against the cold marble table to support my "weak knees." While trying to think up something less caustic, I wondered if I was about to become his next cadaver.

After a reasonable pause, he said, with victory on his face, "Ha! I thought so!" and walked away.

I felt hollow and faithless as if I'd just let God down.

With twenty years of retrospect, I can see how God used that indiscreet and painful confrontation to bolster within me an insatiable desire to speak up often as His witness. But I still do not witness enough. Many times, standing there with a mouth full of teeth instead of praise, I "advertise" for dentistry instead of Christ.

What constitutes a witness? What do we mean by witnessing? Must you take all kinds of witnessing courses? What about just living a life that is a witness? Isn't that important too? If we do talk, what do we say? When do we say it? How do we say it? Undoubtedly you've asked those questions just as I have.

Germane to any witness is a thorough knowledge of the subject material—the Person of Christ—and a heart filled with the Subject Himself. Our living experience must match what we say, and vice versa. Therefore, this book includes several chapters about Christ, faith, the Holy Spirit, and the Scriptures. The better we understand these fundamental concepts, the more articulate and persuasive our communication of the gospel will become. I trust that my explanation of these truths will generate ideas for your own sharing of them.

Witnessing courses may be very helpful to begin with, but prewritten presentations of Christ often hinder *our* input; therefore, they are less than a sparkling reflection of our exciting and personal Savior as He radiates His love to you and me—individually. Preestablished tools sometimes prevent us from taking our contacts seriously, unnecessarily turning away offended people.

We may be alike anatomically, but by the grace of God our personalities and spirits are very different. There's as much variation in our ability to witness as in our personality potential. God sees no two of us alike. Each of us is an original creation, with unique skills for serving Him and with abilities that carry deeper responsibilities every year we live close to Him. If we live apart from Him, the consequences grow proportionately more severe. We are all witnesses to something! God tells us that we are either for Him or against Him, we are either scattering or gathering. There is no middle ground. Neutrality does not exist with God.

Throughout this book I quote from Scripture. When I insert my editorial comments within a scriptural quote, my words are set off with brackets: [—].

1

The Rainbow—Jesus Christ

After the wedding, the bride and groom stood outside the church. It had been hot and muggy all day; now, toward evening, large, billowing, black thunderheads were rising in the west, nearly obscuring the sunset.

As the line of well-wishers continued to pass by the bride and groom, my wife and I noticed a complete rainbow in the east. I remember how others, still in line, nudged one another to draw their attention to it. Soon everyone admired the rainbow, including the bride and groom.

Jesus Christ is a rainbow of far greater beauty in the life of the Christian, and every Christian carries an obligation to point others to Him. We always show off rainbows, don't we? Why are we so faithful to a rainbow in the sky and so shy to point to our Savior? I met a man who presented Jesus Christ to absolutely everyone he met, without exception. His faithfulness was unique. I met him (I'd like to refer to him as a "stranger") on a jet.

The engines were being revved up one at a time, until all four whirred. Then, as if the pilot had pulled an emergency lever, they were all shut down, and the passenger gateway was reextended to the plane. In rushed our stranger. His suit looked as if he had been sleeping in it for two days! His shirt was halfway out of his pants, his tie was loose, and his head was topped off with a red golfer's cap that sat crookedly on his messed-up, graying hair. He ran down the aisle with bags, camera, books, and other paraphernalia, and wouldn't you know it—he decided to splatter himself and his baggage in the seat next to me. I was sitting along the aisle so he had to fall all over me to get in. Why me? The plane was half empty.

For a while, he just sat there with his silly cap perched on his head, catching his breath, but the wheels of the jet hadn't lifted off the runway in Atlanta, Georgia, before he introduced himself. He did so with such gusto, and so loudly, that I was embarrassed. Everyone on the plane must have been able to hear him! We talked a bit. He discovered that I had come from Michigan via O'Hare airport in Chicago; and I learned that he actually had been in his wrinkled suit for the past forty-eight hours, traveling from China via Hong Kong, Japan, Los Angeles, and Atlanta. Both of us were now enroute to Orlando, Florida—together.

We probably were near fifteen thousand feet on our way up to thirty-three thousand when he popped his black and very worn Bible in my face, saying, "Excuse me again, but I don't have my glasses on. Would you mind looking up 1 John 1:9 for me?" Pulling my head back far enough to get my nose out of the pages, I took the Bible from him, then slid three inches farther into the seat—just in case anyone behind me was watching.

I wondered why he didn't just put his glasses on instead of bugging me. Maybe he sat on them somewhere along the way! How did he know that I could find 1 John 1:9? I read the text to him and began to hand his Bible back. He pushed it into my hands once more and had at least a dozen other passages for me to look up and read. It soon became apparent that he was witnessing to me directly from the Scriptures, without editorial comment. This was his way of introducing Jesus Christ to everyone he met—strangers or not.

Having no questions about God's plan of salvation, I simply confirmed the fact that we had the Person of Christ in common and offered to take him home in a rented car I had reserved ahead. The trip was supposed to be only fifty miles long, over good roads, but it took us twenty-four hours because of the breakdowns—none of which had anything to do with the car. This benevolent character had an unbelievable vocation: He confronted every stranger we came upon during that evening and the next day, including every hitchhiker. He witnessed to them until *they* broke down.

I lost count of the number of "breakdowns" we encountered. Each thumbing traveler had to be shoved into the back seat of the rented economy car. If I had known he did this to everyone, I would have rented a larger car—maybe even a bus. I had never before met so many strangers in one short trip.

During the night and early hours of morning, five prayed to receive Jesus Christ. Just as the sun was rising, we picked up a young man about eighteen years old. He absolutely refused to read from the Bible. He just wouldn't. It soon became apparent that he couldn't. He had never learned to read; so we read the Bible to him for about twenty minutes. He accepted Jesus Christ with the most beautiful, humble, and sincere prayer I have ever heard.

What a joy to see this stranger at work for the Lord, frustrating the devil in the power of the Holy Spirit. Chills ran down my back, listening to him present Jesus Christ so boldly and aggressively, using his unique personality to do it. What an explosive Christian!

Many of us would give up when comparing ourselves to this dynamo; therefore, we must be aware that God has a specific purpose for each of us. If He didn't, we wouldn't be here, for God's Word tells us that He knew us before birth (Jer. 1:5; Ps. 129:13–24). Exactly what God's plan is for your life, He will tell *you* since one thing is certain: His plan is individually tailored for you and for no one else. He does not want us to compare ourselves with someone else. God deals with us in the same way He brought us into the world. From literally hundreds of thousands of sperm cells, God saw to it that one, and only one, fertilized the egg in your mother's womb that particular month (even day and hour) when you were conceived. You are you, and there's no one else like you—now, ever before, or in the future.

Because you are unique, God has a special plan for the personality He gave you. We have no business comparing ourselves with another of God's creation, especially if we use that comparison to draw an erroneous conclusion that we are "worthless" when it comes to witnessing. God wants to use each of us through our individual personalities, but because we don't always remember this, witnessing has become an area of failure, even among dedicated Christians. We often become so frustrated that we don't even want to think about it anymore, let alone learn how to reflect Christ effectively. We argue against the need to witness, completely forgetting God's reminder that we are witnessing either for Him or against Him by our very existence. There's no in-between (Matt. 12:30).

A lady once told me that Jesus "gave some to be apostles, some to be prophets, some to be evangelists, and some to be pastors and teachers" (Eph. 4:11). She concluded from this passage that these experts are supposed to do the witnessing while she and the rest of us—businessmen, professional people, housewives, factory workers, and salesmen—really cannot master a witness. I didn't have a clear-cut answer for her at the time, but I do now. I'll share it with you later, but first, let me tell you about hitchhiker number nine.

This one had a hard time getting into the back seat of our small car. He was tall, good-looking, and about nineteen years old. I hadn't shifted through second gear yet when the Bible sailed into the back seat. "Will you look up 1 John 1:9 for me, please? I don't have my glasses on." After he said it, the stranger waited for the hitchhiker's response. The hitchhiker just sat there bewildered. I remember becoming concerned that he might be on drugs. He was asked again, and this time the response was unmistakable irritability. For the third time the hitchhiker was pressed for 1 John 1:9. This time his disgust turned to outright contempt. The hitchhiker wasn't in a mood to read anything, let alone a passage out of the Bible. Speaking for the first time, he let both of us know it. Obviously this man wasn't searching. He was being confronted, and he didn't like it one bit.

"Here—take this back—read it yourself. I'm not your servant!"

"No, you just hold it for a while. Tell me, do you know Jesus Christ?"

"Whatcha talkin' about man? Get off my back. I didn't ask for this!"

"All I am asking you is, Do you know Jesus?"

"Hey, you guys Holy Rollers or somethin'!? Get lost!"

"If you don't know Him, son, I'd like to introduce you to Him right now."

This brought a rash of cursing, a command to stop the car, and vulgarities. As the stranger prodded the hitchhiker further, both of us were threatened. His face reddened and his eyes became violent. "Shut up, damn it, shut up!" he screamed. Then in one sweep, he picked up the Bible (still closed) from the seat and hurled it into the windshield of the car, just missing the stranger's face. Then he offered to kill us both.

I was ready to "shake the dust from my feet." They were shaking anyway! But our stranger had other ideas. He spun around in the front seat like a bolt of lightning. He was on his knees with his chest against the back of the seat, eyeball to eyeball with the fuming hitchhiker. Almost before the Bible could fall to the floor, our stranger said, "In the name of Jesus Christ, I command you, devil, leave this boy!"

I don't know who was more shocked, the hitchhiker or me. After a long half-minute of silence (it seemed more like a half-hour), the boy shouted back, "I don't need you. I found power, man!"

"What kind of power do you have, son? Who gave it to you?"

"Damn you, I don't have to tell you anything! Now let me outta here!"

I remember wondering, Is this why I had rented a compact car? We had this kid captive in our two-door. The stranger took full advantage of this fact and pushed the confrontation still further—far beyond the boiling point. "Who gave you your power?"

"God did, that's who!"

"No, He did not. Jesus gives power. Only Jesus could have given you power through His Holy Spirit. Did you get it from Jesus? Say Jesus. Say His wonderful name. Say Jesus!"

"Go to hell!"

"No, that's where you're going. That's where you came from, and that's where you belong! Devil, get away from this boy!" he shouted. Then in a near whisper, he added, "Son,

I'm not yelling at you. I'm talking to the devil who has control of you."

With both knees firmly planted in the front seat, he stretched his arms out, placed them on the shoulders of the boy, and screamed with a deafening shout, "In the name of Jesus Christ, I command you, devil, leave this boy alone!"

"Say Jesus, say His wonderful name."

"Sir, I would like to leave. May I get out of here, please?"

"No, I won't let you go. I won't leave you alone."

Suddenly the boy's body fell limp. The violence that was in his eyes disappeared. Obviously, something had happened. He looked bewildered. A tear began to form in his eye, then one in mine. He hung his head for a second. Then lifting his face toward the sky, he wept: "OHHhhh Jesus, OHHHhhhh Jesus, Jesus, Jesus, Jesus . . . help me Jesus."

The dialogue that followed was with a "different person." The hitchhiker told us that he had really wanted to believe Christ earlier, even that night, but that he never could comprehend. We told him what Paul said about that: "The man without the Spirit does not accept the things that come from the Spirit of God, for they are foolishness to him, and he cannot understand them, because they are spiritually discerned" (1 Cor. 2:14). Then we started through the Old Testament and pointed to Jesus there.

Although confrontation, of the sort that our stranger used, may not be commanded of us by God, eager availability in pointing others to Jesus Christ is required. That's why we must clean up the "mud puddles" of our lives. Then His rainbow of love can better be reflected in us at all times; otherwise our contacts will have all kinds of trouble understanding what the gospel means. Let me develop more carefully this definition of witnessing as a reflection of Jesus in each of our lives.

2

Witnessing—
___ A Personality Extension

Witnessing for Jesus Christ is an expression, or an extension, of Christ's personality through us, regardless of our strong or weak points. A rainbow is best reflected in a still and quiet puddle, especially a mud puddle. If we've completely yielded, we'll maintain a calm reflection of Christ in our everyday lives.

Perhaps the most confusing aspect of witnessing is the lack of a universal method, one which everyone can easily assimilate and comfortably use. Some methods come close to full acceptance, but even they must be supplemented by individual personalities to one degree or another—a necessary ingredient to any witness. Because God uses each of us as He made us, methods are ultimately as varied as people. Witnessing, inescapably, is a matter of sharing oneself.

Witnessing Is Not Sharing Christ

Perhaps we should get some terminology straight right from the start. We speak of "sharing Christ" and "sharing our faith." This cannot be done. I cannot distribute my faith; neither can you. I need every bit of my faith for myself. Furthermore, it has my name written all over it. Likewise, "sharing Christ" sounds nice enough, but it's an inaccurate assumption.

Remember the parable of the ten virgins Jesus taught us? The wise virgins were asked by the foolish virgins to share their oil. The wise virgins refused saying, "Lest there be not enough for us and you" (Matt. 25:9, KJV). It's the same with our faith. We need all we've got! We don't parcel out Christ or our faith.

Witnessing is an *implantation* of Jesus Christ into the heart of another through the operation of the Holy Spirit. Certainly implanting denotes activity on our part; however, the entire operation is fundamentally that of the Holy Spirit as opposed to our generosity in sharing.

As Christians, we are divinely compelled to witness. This was the point I tried to make to the lady who didn't want to witness (referred to in the first chapter). Whether we are apostles, housewives, prophets, professional men, evangelists, salesmen, pastors, students, teachers, or a stranger from China, we must all point others to Christ—the object, means, and source of all saving faith.

The issues are tricky. Our mandate to witness may not be handed off to anyone else, not even to the Holy Spirit. The responsibility is ours; yet in God's divine plan, the Holy Spirit performs the work of regeneration in the heart of the unbeliever. He has chosen to accomplish His work through us as Christians, but God does not really need us!

In Luke 19:40, Jesus said He could use stones to cry out for Him. Imagine a sandy beach, each grain of sand crying out, "Jesus Christ is Lord!" God told Abraham that his offspring would number as the sands on the shore. Why then are we not crying out, "Jesus Christ is Lord"? If God needs us, it is only because He planned it that way. *We* are the offspring about whom God was talking. Why aren't we out gathering? Are we afraid to trust His Spirit to accomplish His commission? Are we afraid we may fail when there *are no* failures in witnessing?

Our Mandate to Witness

The very topic of reflecting Jesus Christ in our mud puddles—witnessing—turns off the lukewarm Christian. Some may nearly leave the communion of the saints over differences of opinion raised on the subject.

Jesus Himself gave us our mandate to witness: "Therefore go and make disciples of all nations, baptizing them in the name of the Father and of the Son and of the Holy Spirit, and teaching them to obey everything I have commanded you. And surely I will be with you always, to the very end of the age" (Matt. 28:19–20).

Many times before our Lord actually engages us in His work, He first tells us: "Do your best to present yourself to God as one approved, a workman who does not need to be ashamed and who correctly handles the word of truth" (2 Tim. 2:15). In other words, the Lord's first desire is that we master His Word so that when we do witness for Him we will handle it correctly and accurately. Often, God will have one of us "stay . . . until you have been clothed with power from on high" (Luke 24:49).

These periods of study and waiting could hardly be termed a cop-out; they are not even procrastinating. Too many of us *have* nearly mastered an understanding of the plan of salvation as presented in Scripture and *have* been clothed with power from God; yet we never seem to get started. We may spin our wheels a little bit, but we never get any place in witnessing for Christ because we've become experts at stalling instead. Are you a procrastinator against Christ instead of a witness for him? I was for over half my life!

Procrastinators Frustrate the Reflection of Jesus' Personality

A procrastinator is one who would rather postpone witnessing for Christ until the "next time," then procrastinate some more. You can usually identify a procrastinator by his watch—set at least ten minutes ahead so that he's on time, at least some of the time. Even though most procrastinators are totally unreliable when it comes to being on time, you can always count on finding them last in line, just before midnight, every April 15, mailing in their income tax returns— on time.

When Christ was asked about paying taxes to Caesar, He replied: "Give to Caesar what is Caesar's, and to God what is God's" (Matt. 22:31). The government has a way of usurping our free will to procrastinate when it comes to paying taxes, but God allows us to exercise it when challenged to witness for Him.

Therefore, when it comes to witnessing for our Lord, I recognize at least five groups of habitual procrastinators; and worse than that, I recognize a little of myself in each group. Let's consider all five groups.

The first group consists of those who feel they are too unworthy to make bold His worthiness. The second group hides under the table; they are far too insecure in their own faith to tell anyone else about it. The third group simply refuses to think about witnessing, let alone talk about it. (I classify these people as pseudo-Christians.) Those in the fourth group back away, feeling that someone else can do it better. Those in the fifth group are convinced they are already proclaiming the famous "silent witness."

Some serious hazards lurk in all these postures. Those in the first group (the unworthy) are sincerely concerned with their sin-status. They feel so rotten that they pronounce themselves unworthy to reflect Jesus or even talk about "conversion" to someone else since conversion means a turning *away* from sin and its memories. How can *they* witness for Christ when their sin-consciousness is so immediate?

These people accept the doctrine of total depravity to the point of total ineffectiveness. They completely overlook the fantastic comfort and assurance given all sinners in 1 John 1:9: "If we confess our sins, he is faithful and just and will forgive us our sins and purify us from all unrighteousness."

A Christian who continues in this mistaken belief says in effect, "Christ may have paid it all, but I still fail. I am too unworthy." These people would like to receive forgiveness for sins committed, but they also want to punish themselves. They witness against Christ because Christ suffered all the punishment necessary to rid us of our sins. Once our sins are forgiven, we dare not wear them as a badge of dishonor or use them as an "excuse" not to reflect the Forgiver.

Can't you just imagine how Paul would enjoy talking to these people? He admitted that he was the chief of sinners; yet he witnessed for Christ even while conceding that! He said, "Christ Jesus came into the world to save sinners—of whom I am the worst" (1 Tim. 1:15). Paul always emphasized the victory of Christ, not his own defeat.

Those in the second group (the insecure) want to "play it safe." They feel much too irresolute to enter the nasty, sin-sick world. They would rather retreat into spiritual isolation, becoming spiritual ants instead of spiritual giants. By withdrawing from the world of sin, these people actually permit the devil to have exclusive misuse rights in certain areas of sin. They turn their righteous backs on the unrighteous rather than involving themselves in a witness for Jesus Christ. They are actually witnessing against Him!

Our Lord knows how sinful the world is. He sent us into this rotten mess to reflect His light, and He sent us in with a prayer. This is the petition Jesus offered to His Father for the people in the second group: "My prayer is not that you take them out of the world but that you protect them from the evil one. They are not of the world, even as I am not of it. Sanctify them by the truth; your word is truth. As you sent me into the world, I have sent them into the world. For them I sanctify myself, that they too may be truly sanctified" (John 17:15–19). The treatment for insecurity is a large dose of sanctification, which comes from repeated exposure to Scripture, three, four, or five times daily.

The third group of procrastinators is the most complex and difficult to understand. They absolutely *refuse* to witness for Jesus and *deliberately* avoid the subject of Christ. These pseudo-Christians are all around us, acting like real Christians. Like the fig tree with no figs, just a lot of leaves, they are role-players. There is no fruit, just show. They are enemies of the cross, not because they refuse to witness for Christ, but because they still have not received the baptism of the Holy Spirit. They are not yet redeemed! Let me hastily add that these people are not those who believe in the so-called silent witness.

Pseudo-Christians have no idea of the joy involved in witnessing because they have rejected Him who is joy. Without Christ, they end up totally frustrated whenever witnessing comes up, feeling threatened rather than privileged. Often, they are cozily protected by well-meaning Christians who suggest that we should not overemphasize the verbalization of one's faith since it only further irritates them into pure panic. I agree that we shouldn't talk to them about witnessing. We should witness *to* them, for they are not committed Christians.

Granted, some people have difficulty communicating; I'm not referring to them. The phony Christian holds his own loud and clear when someone short-changes him; he can hoot and holler at sporting events, and he talks up a storm about sports or children. He does not lack the ability to speak even as some pretend; rather, his problem is a lack of interest in and a lack of commitment to the Person of Jesus Christ!

Perhaps it should be reemphasized: Pseudo-Christians are *routinely* frustrated and *constantly* threatened by the thought of witnessing for Jesus. We all have "off" days, but pseudo-Christians distinguish themselves by making every day an "off" day.

My harshness is scriptural. The Bible says this positively: "If anyone acknowledges that Jesus is the Son of God, God lives in him and he in God" (1 John 4:15). This means that those who do not witness or confess Jesus to others do not have God living in them and they do not dwell in God. That's why we must mark them as pseudo-Christians.

Someday, a well-meaning Christian will figuratively sneak up behind one of these quiet, reserved, nonexcitable nonwitnesses and jab him with something sharp. I can hear the beautiful exultation already! Instead of writing these people off, let's pray that God will do exactly that with the sword of His Spirit. Paul told us this could happen: "The word of God is living and active [powerful]. Sharper than any double-edged sword, it penetrates even to dividing soul and spirit, joints and marrow; it judges the thoughts and attitudes of the heart" (Heb. 4:12).

Witnessing is not only an evidence of our salvation but an evidence of our spiritual health. As long as those in the third group aren't physically dead, there is still hope.

The fourth group consists of those who honestly feel that someone else could do it better. If this is really true, it only indicates a lack of preparation. God gave each of us a unique personality and a mandate to use that personality in witnessing for Him. We really have no right to pass off to someone else God's peculiar expectation of us.

These people like to think of themselves as "neutral" since they believe they are doing nothing *wrong* by doing nothing. They disregard Christ's statement that "he who is not with me is against me, and he who does not gather with me scatters" (Matt. 12:30). Perhaps they are best classified as lukewarm. But God warns, even promises, that He will spit them out of His mouth (see Rev. 3:15).

Jesus also directed our attention to this matter: "Whosoever shall deny [disown] me before men, him will I also deny [disown] before my Father which is in heaven" (Matt. 10:33, KJV). Surely, if we, by virtue of our inactivity, are against Him, then we are denying Him, and He will finally deny us.

The procrastinators in the fifth group maintain that their special talent is the "silent witness." This has some merit but only some. Peter addressed himself to the fifth group: ". . . in your hearts acknowledge Christ as the holy Lord [but] always be prepared to give an answer to everyone who asks you to give the reason for the hope that you have" (1 Pet. 3:15).

Have you noticed that persons enthused about a specific

aspect of their lives relate nearly every experience to that particular subject? Take flying as an example. You can hardly say to a pilot "It's a nice day today" without causing him to think about weather fronts, highs and lows, visibility, and cloud cover or ceilings. It's the same with the person filled with (therefore enthused about) Christ. He can hardly hear a mundane statement without giving it a spiritual reference. I heard a man take a simple fact and turn it into a witnessing opportunity just because he related everything to spiritual matters. It seems that a woman had lost her mother early in life. The mother was only twenty-three when she died. The woman had already outlived her mother by forty years. The listener merely asked, "I wonder what it will be like in heaven to have a mother half your age?"

When Jesus Christ becomes ultimate in our lives, every situation, every happening, every conversation, is related and compared with Him. Too often, however, these thoughts—placed in our consciousness by the Holy Spirit—are allowed to dissolve without verbal expression. They drift off as a stifled "silent witness." No one will ever hear of the saving power of Jesus Christ simply by observing us go silently through life!

Have you been brought face to face with yourself in any of these five groups of procrastinators? I've been involved with enough "logic" in each of their arguments to make me shudder. I've felt too unworthy, too insecure. At one time, I even wanted to put an end to my overt witnessing forever, feeling others could surely do it better. I'd just be content with the simple life, the silent witness, I said. I've been there!

Because I had been outspoken for Christ ever since my human anatomy fiasco in dental school, I had many possibilities for outreach. After only two years of private practice,

Charles Van Dyken, Jr., D.D.S. (in private practice himself only three years) presented me with an irresistible witnessing challenge: "Let's establish a dental clinic on a major mission field and serve as short term volunteers for the missionaries in the hope that this will save a few of their teeth." Missionaries who serve in Africa usually came home only once in every three years, and their dental appointments consisted mostly of extractions. This was an unnecessary waste.

So, after sending a contractor ahead to install the new donated dental equipment, we spent six weeks in the "sauna" of Africa's heat working on 110 of the missionary personnel and 55 natives from the staff at Takum Christian Hospital in northern Nigeria, taking over 210 X rays and filling a total of 570 teeth; only to be informed by the missionaries that this was not a good witness in itself. I would have thought that the beads of perspiration running down our backs and dripping off the ends of our noses would have counted for something but there were countless curious Africans—not sweating a bit—wanting to have their teeth "washed." The news of what we had done for the native staff had spread like wildfire and soon the lines began to form outside the dental clinic. Some of these good people had traveled five or six days on calloused feet to visit us. We were guests in their country, so we polished the betel nut stain off their teeth from sunup to sundown for the last two weeks while the lines grew longer every day. Our "improved" witness was still frustrated because of the language barrier. So we learned how to say "Jesus" in both the Tiv and Hausa languages, and when they would try to thank us, we'd just point toward Heaven and say "Jesus" in both languages to be sure each understood the motive.

Two years later, I became involved in another project

called "Friendly Town"—transporting needy children from Harlem, New York, to western Michigan for a two week vacation. Then in late 1967, I became involved in radio and television marathons from coast to coast raising funds to send "Thank You Packets," with New Testaments in them, to every man on the front lines of Vietnam.

The international recognition of "Project Thank You" netted an unusual request: Would I contribute my Christian witness to a new movie company in Hollywood? What a chance for outreach! This had to be God's will for my life, I reasoned. I didn't bother to ask Him if it really was, and at that moment I headed for certain failure! I had taken cognizance of God's extraordinary blessings to me and somehow translated these into *my* inherent ability. That made me a sitting duck for God to shoot down—and He did! I leaped headlong into the film business. I hadn't stopped praying, but my prayers became "progress reports" rather than resting periods when I surrendered my will to His will and waited for guidance. I was on the road to actual disaster, my first, not realizing that in essence I had already arrived.

Tumultuous months followed. Because of God's grace and my sheer determination, a full-length Hollywood Christian film was finally completed and premiered as *The Ballad of Billie Blue*. For all the incredible effort and expense, I still had a picture that was too worldly for the Christian and too Christian for the world! Nevertheless, I couldn't quit. I had the investors' money to protect. Throw in the towel? Not after two years of praying! I wondered, nevertheless, why God had apparently pulled the plug on my prayers! Wasn't this supposed to be a witness for *Him*? Perhaps it was originally; but now everything was twisted out of shape, and so was my faith. I finally had to admit failure. Crushed by a series of tragic mistakes, I felt like never witnessing overtly again.

I praise God that out of those ashes He drew me closer to His love and forgiveness. He had pulverized my "free spirit," led me to a film distributor, refocused my total attention toward Him, and gave me His Spirit of peace. My unworthiness was soon dissipated in Scripture. I exchanged my sense of insecurity for God's surety and began thinking of a *real* witness for Christ.

I studied the Bible as never before, trying to learn all I could about Jesus—His witness, His personality, His disciples, their personalities. What kind of characters did He handpick to be His disciples? Could any of them have been as stupid as I?

Let's take a closer look at Christ—the *faithful* witness—and at His pupils—the disciples and how He taught *them*.

3

Jesus As Teacher and Preacher— The Faithful Witness

In His teaching, Jesus was unique. The only source material He used was Old Testament Scripture. He quoted it without mutilation. He didn't invent a new theology; yet He so impressed His students that they often said in admiration, "This is a new teaching."

Because Christ was the Messiah, He was His own central theme. He presented Himself as the solution. Most psychologists will agree that this approach would be destined for disaster. Historians can point to several men who have tried such a method and failed. Jesus' focus on Himself was not original; yet no one before or since has succeeded in becoming the universal "answer." That makes Jesus the original teacher-preacher indeed!

His method of teaching was primordial; yet He added to and amplified the Old Testament. He added by changing the point of emphasis. When referring to the teachings of Moses, He usually followed with, "But *I* say unto you . . ." then He drew fresh and stringent applications. As a teacher, His human and divine natures were inseparable but distinguishable. Because we can differentiate His dual nature (a factor we will examine in the next chapter), we can discover how He witnessed on a person-to-person basis. What would Christ have us learn from His personality to augment an understanding of our role in witnessing? Basically that our Lord's humanness prompted Him to move with *compassion*. This human quality initiated the teaching session recorded in Mark. "When Jesus landed and saw a large crowd, he had compassion on them, because they were like sheep without a shepherd. So he began teaching them many things" (Mark 6:34).

God, in His wisdom, gave you and me a glimmer of Christ's compassion so that we could develop a similar attitude in our presentations of His plan of salvation. What a crucial point to remember when witnessing to the "hard of heart"!

Jesus' expounding always had the compassionate touch. He took time to explain difficult concepts. Painstakingly, he detailed His teachings for the disciples, for the crowds, and for individuals. He interpreted parables and the Scriptures and patiently made sure His audience caught the point.

Perhaps the greatest test of any teacher and any witness is the ability to transfer knowledge. If you, as a teacher, were to teach a trade successfully, your pupils would duplicate your methods. Christ's disciples were handpicked and taught, by Christ Himself, to witness to others. They did it so well that the world called them *Christ*ians!

The Personality of Jesus Christ Ingrafted into Ours— To Witness for Him

I have noted that all men are not created equal in their ability to witness for Christ. Certain traits in our personalities, either purposefully or accidentally, unfold at the expense of other traits. Even if we had developed only our best qualities, we would still not be fit (of ourselves) to witness. In ourselves there is no "good." We require the ingrafting of Jesus Christ's personality to augment our failure potential. He makes us new creations by His redemptive and indwelling work. Christ works through us, not "instead of us."

Let's look at how He rearranged personality potentials in the past by observing the "failures" He chose to be His disciples. Christ, the faithful witness, taught His disciples to witness. What kinds of men did He choose? What kinds of witnessers did He make out of them? Would you recognize yourself in any of His pupils?

Peter: This fisherman was a weak-kneed individual who could bend like a reed; yet he was made over into a rock! Still, he was Peter all the way. He was naturally impulsive (Matt. 14:28, 17:4; John 21:7). He also showed tenderheartedness and affection (Matt. 26:75; John 13:9, 21:15–17). Packed full of contradictions, he was at times presumptuous (Matt. 16:22; John 13:8, 18:10) and at other times actually a sissy and very timid (Matt. 14:30, 26:69–72). He sacrificed self (Mark 1:18), but he was also inclined to be self-seeking (Matt. 19:27). Peter was gifted with spiritual insight (John 6:68); still, he was slow to learn and sluggish in comprehending the deeper truths (Matt. 15:15–16). He made two fantastic confessions of faith (Matt. 16:16; John 6:69); but true to his ability to contradict himself, he also made the greatest denial (Mark 14:67–71). Peter was rash (John 18:10–11), conceited (Matt. 26:33), lazy (Matt. 26:40), and blasphemous (Mark 14:70–71). It wasn't until after the resurrection and Pentecost (the ingrafting of the Holy Spirit) that Peter became the "rock" (John 1:42; Matt. 16:18; Acts 1:8). He became courageous and immovable (Acts 4:19–20; 5:28, 29, 40, 42). He was also patient and understanding and able to take harsh criticism from Paul and still love him. When we look at Peter, we should be better able to understand that after one is *in* Christ and Christ is *in* him he becomes "a new creature." God ingrafts Christ's personality into ours in order to strengthen our witness for Him.

John: Here is the *beloved disciple.* What more can one say? What a fantastic thing to be called by your Lord. What an honor! It would seem almost a distraction to add anything to that description, but there are reasons John was the beloved disciple. He was full of energy (Mark 3:17) and was called a son of thunder; yet he was still John and intolerant of "outsiders" doing the Lord's work (Mark 9:38). He was vindictive (Luke 9:54) in wanting the Samaritans consumed by fire. He was ambitious (Mark 10:35–37) and even presumptuous when he and James asked to sit at either hand of Christ in heaven, but John's personality was modified through his association with Jesus. Christ grafted compassion into him (John 13:23; 1 John 2:10, 3:14–18, 4:7–11) and entrusted John with the care of His mother, Mary (John 19:26).

James: This apostle was John's brother and was also called a son of thunder. James and John the fishermen, sons of Zebedee, immediately dropped their nets and followed Him (Matt. 4:21), but this does not mean that they believed in Him immediately (John 7:5). Even though we do not know *when* (which is never as important as *if*) James accepted Christ, the significant thing is that he did take Christ as his Lord and Savior. Later he was one of the magnificent and sensitive leaders of the church at Jerusalem (Acts 15:13, 21:18).

Andrew: A person-to-person worker, Andrew was a soul-winner for the kingdom. He was also the brother of Peter; so we might expect to find some similar tendencies between them. Both were fishermen (Matt. 4:18), but the affinities seem to stop there. Andrew was a disciple of John the Baptist (John 1:35, 40), but he did spend a day in Jesus' "house" (John 1:39). Like James and John, Andrew dropped his net immediately and followed Jesus (Matt. 4:19–20). After he learned from the teacher-preacher and received Christ's power, he first brought his brother Peter to Jesus (John 1:40–42), demonstrating that "mission work" and witnessing always begin at home.

Philip: This disciple was slow to comprehend; yet he was handpicked by Jesus. Philip seemed to learn best through questioning; he was one to want physical proof (John 14:6–14). All teachers give exams, and Jesus tested Philip. When Jesus saw the five thousand approaching, He said to Philip, "Where shall we buy bread for these people to eat?" (John 6:5). It's no surprise that Philip "flunked the test" (John 6:8) because his only point of reference was materialistically conceived. He obviously needed more implanting of Christ's person before being prepared to carry forth the Great Commission.

Matthew: If there ever was a publican with a purpose and mission in life, it was Matthew. His entire Gospel focuses on the Jew and is written to emphasize that Jesus Christ *fulfilled* the Old Testament prophecies. He talks about the king and the kingdom of heaven throughout his Gospel. Although he was a tax collector who left everything to follow Jesus, Matthew never stopped being uniquely Matthew. He prepared a great feast for our Lord. Jesus attended in spite of the fact that Matthew was a publican (Luke 5:29). Christ punched His witness home to the Jews through this disciple more than any other because He uses each of us as we are when we allow Him to ingraft Himself into us as a source of power—His power, not ours. Matthew the tax collector was transformed into a Christ-centered preacher for fifteen years. His personality was not changed but refocused. When you read God's holy and word-by-word inspired Bible, you can see the way God maintained the uniquely individualist personality of each Gospel writer. Matthew is only one such example. The biblical authors remained themselves and wrote as they spoke; yet God inspired every one of *their* (and His) words.

Thomas: This doubter was close to Christ (John 11:16), and he was devoted; but, like Philip, he was a pokey learner. Unsure of his own responsibility to witness, he asked many questions of his Teacher. "Lord, we don't know where you are going, so how can we know the way?" (John 14:5). This is a reasonable question considering the amount of knowledge the Lord had given the disciples prior to Pentecost. Somehow Thomas was looking the other way or was completely absent from "school" the day Christ arose and appeared (John 20:24). He, therefore, doubted the whole thing (John 20:25). Thomas was given indisputable evidence (John 20:27), and *then* he made his confession of faith (John 20:28). The skeptic was convinced and then could witness as a converted doubter to other vacillators, but he was still Thomas.

Judas Iscariot: The betrayer of Jesus was nevertheless Jesus' friend. Jesus said a lot of things about loving your enemies, blessing those who curse you, and turning the other cheek, but He did even more: He demonstrated His compassionate friendship under adverse conditions. Judas was called friend by Jesus both directly and indirectly. Jesus forthrightly addressed Judas as friend in the garden of Gethsemane *after* Judas had kissed Him (Matt. 26:49–50)!

Calling Judas friend was not a mistake or a word spoken without much thought.

In John's Gospel we read: "He who shares my bread has lifted up his heel against me" (John 13:18). Jesus said those words for everyone to hear. He recited them from the Old Testament: "Yea, mine own familiar friend, in whom I trusted, which did eat of my bread, hath lifted up his heel against me" (Ps. 41:9, KJV).

In the psalms David was writing about his personal friend Ahithophel (2 Sam. 1:12), but Jesus used this text to refer to Judas and His own betrayal. The linkage is permissible, for it is this portion of Holy Scripture (including the word *friend*) that Jesus referred to when He said, "This is to fulfill the scripture" (John 13:18). Jesus called His betrayer a friend as another example of His compassion in dealing with others.

Judas was avaricious. He demonstrated greed (Matt. 26:14–15) and hypocrisy (John 12:5–6). Judas was guilty of treachery (Mark 14:10; Luke 22:47–48) and was dishonest in many ways (John 12:6). He also displayed remorse (Matt. 27:3–4; Acts 1:18).

James, the son of Alphaseus, *Thaddaeus*, *Simon*, the Canaanite, and *Bartholomew* we know too little about to compare their personalities before and after they knew our Lord.

Paul: Although Paul was not one of the twelve, he was nevertheless a disciple of our Lord and was taught to witness. A man of many visions, Paul saw a vision of Christ (Acts 18:9). He also saw the visions of warning (Acts 22:18), work (Acts 23:11), encouragement in the midst of storm (Acts 27:33), and heaven (2 Cor. 12:1–4). His very obedience to these revelations formed Paul's characteristic personality and explain his fabulous witnessing career (Acts 26:19). Paul was joy (Acts 16:25; 2 Cor. 6:10, 7:4; Phil. 4:4), courage (Acts 16:36–37; 22:25; 24:25), steadfastness (Acts 20:24), earnest (Acts 20:31; Rom. 9:3; Phil. 3:18), industrious (Acts 20:34; 1 Tim. 2:9), tactful (1 Cor. 9:19–22), faithful (2 Tim. 4:7–8), patient (2 Cor. 12:12), and full of love and compassion (1 Cor. 16:24; 2 Cor. 2:4).

It must be pointed out, however, that before Paul met our Savior he was a full-time enemy of God. He crusaded vigorously against God's people. He was easily angered and often intolerant; yet he was handpicked by God.

God accepts us right "where we're at" and then changes us into faithful witnesses for Him by ingrafting in us a new life—His life—and expressing it through our redeemed and refined personalities. God does not give us Christ's personality in exchange for ours. Jesus didn't make another "little Jesus" out of each disciple. That would have only produced robots or puppets. He gave new life to those personality traits already there, stripping them of sin's effect and enabling them to develop in the power of the Holy Spirit.

Let's look at Jesus' human personality features in comparison with similar, but underdeveloped, traits found in His disciples. Humanly speaking, He had all the liveliness of Peter, without improper gaiety. Jesus had the seriousness of John but without intolerance and vindictiveness. Like Philip, our Lord was a problem solver, but His solutions endured eternally. Paul was "all things to all men," and so was Jesus. Jesus demonstrated the calmness of James, but He did not let it dissipate into apathy. Our Lord showed all the vigor and intenseness of Paul but without violence.

Jesus Christ was merciful but demanded justice; He was courageous but not rash; He was tender but masculine; He was strong but gentle; although He needed no forgiveness Himself, He forgave! Doesn't that make you want to go out and tell others about Him?

Successful witnessing lies in the *act* itself, not primarily in the results. If you arrange two magnets in one way, they will attract each other. If you hide one magnet under the table, you can make the other one on top of the table follow or jump, depending on which way you approach it. In an analogous sense, we can understand the witness of our Lord. He could make people jump or follow. Success in witnessing is never measured by immediate results or conversions. Witnessing is not necessarily winning souls to Christ; it's clearly exposing people to Him.

Naturally, everyone to whom we witness will not accept Christ. This is nothing new; nor is it our fault. Many in Christ's day didn't recognize or accept Him either, and He stood right in front of them! Nor did I immediately recognize Christ's real love and presence through my movie experience, and He was right there all the time, breaking my will so that His grace could be seen and actually saving the film!

Today, in spite of all *my* errors, *The Ballad of Billie Blue* is being blessed by God. Gateway Films of Valley Forge, Pennsylvania, not only stood with me, but reedited the film and made it available in sixteen millimeter as well. We expect it to receive prime-time television exposure. It is being requested as a community rental film, not only in this country, but in different parts of the world. Many have been converted as God has used it, but, before that could happen, I had to step down so that God could take over. That was difficult also because I appeared in the film as the preacher! God is using that witness for *His* glory now, not mine! My glory is in His grace through my failure.

Before we get too carried away with condemning those who don't always recognize our Savior, or condemning ourselves for not witnessing "better," let's explore human nature for what it is. Suppose you lived two thousand years ago with all of the mundane headaches that face you today. Suppose you also had difficulty making ends meet financially and that a few creditors were beginning to threaten you. Picture yourself at work with your bookkeeping—writing checks, paying bills, balancing accounts—and you find yourself short of cash. There is a knock on the door. You open it to find a stranger about thirty years old. He has no credentials, no identification card, no references, and no track record in business affairs; yet He speaks with great authority. He offers to help, and so you let Him in, thinking you might get a piece of the action.

He refuses a fee, promises there will be no hidden charges, and guarantees results. You both move over to the table where the bills are piled up and sit down. He begins the conversation: "Blessed are the poor in spirit," but you only hear the first four words. You smile back and wonder how He knows. He continues: "If someone wants to sue you and take your tunic, let him have your cloak as well."

Your mouth drops open. You are shocked and begin to explain how you have been mistreated by impatient creditors, but He interrupts: "Love your enemies and pray for those who persecute you."

By now you're wondering what kind of business advice this is. Maybe you made a mistake by letting Him in. Perhaps He doesn't understand finances. You try to reintroduce your burden and ask if He is a CPA. He replies: "Do not store up for yourself treasures on earth, where moth and rust destroy, and where thieves break through and steal. For where your treasure is, there your heart will be also!"

Now the point is clear—your values are different from His. Having perceived your thoughts, He quickly adds: "No man can serve two masters. Either he will hate the one and love the other, or he will be devoted to the one and despise the other. You cannot serve both God and money."

Your eyes drop to the bills and back to Him, and you begin to wonder. He interrupts your thoughts once again: "Seek first his kingdom and his righteousness, and all these things will be given to you as well." And He's right!

Can you understand now why some will not recognize or accept our Lord, regardless of how clearly we present Him? What a radically unusual perspective on life! The only failure in witnessing is our refusal to witness.

Jesus—In the Act of Witnessing

Jesus witnessed to sinners, both elect and nonelect, to those who were in and to those who forever would remain outside the kingdom (John 6:54). We often try to select only a few as our prime targets for witnessing and then try to accomplish our task by remote control—sending a "missionary"—forgetting Christ's example to witness at every opportunity.

As a witness, Christ knew Scriptures by virtue of His divinity but also because He was a *student* of the Scriptures. He witnessed in love with authority, (Mark 2:2, 3:10), directness (John 12:26), and tact (Luke 7:45), incorporating examples, illustrations, humor, and even questions into His presentations.

Jesus broke with many traditions of His day. The Jews would have nothing to do with the Samaritans; yet Christ—

a Jew—witnessed to a Samaritan woman at the well. The fact that He even talked to such a despised person puzzled both her (John 4:9) and the disciples (John 4:27). Neither could understand the break with tradition, and both asked Jesus why He did it. The answer was identical with the grounds for breaking with custom today: the salvation of sinners. Our Lord's innovative witness resulted in many more Samaritans believing in Him as Savior and Lord (John 4:41).

Jesus also defied traditional practice when He encountered the scribes and Pharisees. "'Why do your disciples break the tradition of the elders? They don't wash their hands before they eat!' . . . Jesus called the crowd to him and said, 'Listen and understand. What goes into a man's mouth does not make him "unclean," but what comes out of his mouth, that is what makes him "unclean."'" (Matt. 15:2, 10).

Kingdom work is a twenty-four-hour-a-day ministry— traditional or not. Paul said, "Be prepared in season and out of season" (2 Tim. 4:2). Christ would have us be aware of our mission in witnessing. Although His cross has a world-wide dimension (1 John 2:2), He wants us to realize that the whole world is made up of nothing more than a lot of individuals, each of whom has to be confronted—one by one!

Christ's witness was and is directed toward individual hearts. Jesus does not save a world full of people; He saves people full of the world! His mode of handling this includes each of us with our own individual personalities but equipped with Himself.

In order for us accurately to represent this unique Savior, we'll require a thorough knowledge of the complexities surrounding His two natures—human and divine.

4

The Human and Divine
Natures of Christ

Throughout the ages, well-meaning Christians have sought to protect the divinity of our Lord against concentrated efforts to reduce Him to a great man, or even a mere man. Well-meaning Christians have counterattacked by accentuating the divine nature of Christ, thus inadvertently de-emphasizing His human nature. These attacks and counter-attacks have left the entire subject of His human and divine natures more than a little enigmatic. I do not wish to add to the confusion by once again overemphasizing His human-ness. Nevertheless, since our witness constantly centers on Christ, the more we understand about His Person, the more effective our presentation will be.

Jesus Christ is both human and divine (Gal. 4:4; John 1:1); yet both aspects are wrapped up in one Person, in-separable and inextricable. But these natures are distinguish-able, and one cannot deny the existence of either in his wit-ness. The mysterious dual nature of Christ can easily cause confusion, in fact, it has already created centuries of be-wilderment.

Who is Jesus? We speak of Him as a man who felt what

we feel and who was tempted as we are, One with human personality traits similar to ours. Isn't that disrespect?

Perhaps the first and most crucial step is to direct our attention beyond the awe that permeates our sure knowledge that He *is* God. If God the Father wanted us to be so removed—in awe—from a friendship with Jesus, He would not have sent Him as a visible, human God-Person to become our friend as well as our Savior.

A friend is someone you know well, fondly appreciate, and mutually support and who is an ally on your side of the struggle. Jesus is that friend to us. We shouldn't become alarmed that Jesus would be our friend even though He is God (sinless) and we are sinners. Here's what God wants us to understand: "The Son of Man came eating and drinking, and they say, 'Here is a glutton and a drunkard, a friend of tax collectors and "sinners" ' " (Matt. 11:19). As His friends, let us reverently seek to grasp how He, having two natures, can simultaneously be our Friend and Lord.

The mystery of His two natures being inseparable yet distinguishable might be compared to the mystery of the human brain which has two sides. These two sides are anatomically distinguishable yet physically inseparable. The brain as a whole is functionally isolable and measurable. The right side controls the left side of the body, and vice versa. Each half has a different function, as each nature of our Lord's has a different function. We cannot separate the brain into right and left brains and be accurate any more than we can hold to one of Christ's natures and "deny" the other. If we take away one or the other, we have no Christ. Understanding one portion of the human brain does not necessitate dissection of the total head and the patient's death; so the study of one nature of Christ should not disavow His Lordship.

What is the balance between the two natures of our Lord? Fifty-fifty, like the right and left sides of the human brain? That thought is pure foolishness. Jesus is 100 percent God and 100 percent man. Both natures are complete unto themselves. This means that we can explore, understand, and measure His humanity if we have a norm with which to compare it. We have such a standard! God told us that Jesus was just like us except for sin. Our yardstick, therefore, is the very humanity that God gave to sinless Adam before sin distorted it.

When the Scriptures tell us that Jesus was just like us in all things, sin excepted, then Scripture is saying that Christ was just like Adam before the fall. This is tied in nicely with what God accomplished in His plan of salvation. Like Adam, Christ would be tempted, but, unlike Adam, Christ would be victorious over the temptation. Why? If we answer that Christ was God and that's why He didn't sin, we imply that His divine nature supplemented or spilled over into His human nature. This cannot be, and we will see why later. In His humanity and in His divinity, Christ was sinless and perfect. Neither his divinity nor his humanity alone defeated Satan; nor was it a combination of His two natures. Adam was sinless and perfect once too.

To find the answer, let's look more closely at the early days of our Lord's public ministry, His baptism, and the temptation in the desert. God might have been saying in effect, "Let's start where we left off. The devil beat Adam, let's pick it up from there" (see Matt. 4:1–11). The key at this point is the devil's thinking that he had a "fighting chance." The temptation of Jesus Christ was not a cut-and-dried affair. If the trip into the desert was a foregone conclusion, there would have been no temptation or victory.

Here is the core truth: The devil knew who Jesus was. He realized our Lord was both God and man, and still he confronted Jesus with real, strong, authentic temptations. If this were not the case, how could Christ ever say that He was tempted in all things and therefore understood our real temptations (Heb. 4:15)? Jesus was enticed and lived for real. He endured pain during those temptations. "Because he himself suffered when he was tempted, he is able to help those who are being tempted" (Heb. 2:18)! But how did He conquer? If His divine nature did not supplement His human (weaker) nature, how did He win where Adam failed?

Here is the secret: At Jesus' baptism the heavens were opened, "and he saw the Spirit of God descending on him like a dove" (Matt. 3:16). His divinity did not have to flow through His humanity because God added His Spirit to Jesus' human nature! This is not the same as Christ's divine nature, and it is more than Adam had to battle with, but no more than we have. Read 1 Corinthians 10:13.

Rejecting Christ's human victory over temptation jeopardizes the validity of the reconciliation. If Jesus, in His human nature, had to be augmented by His divine nature, did victory over Adam's fall really occur? Not only did Christ conquer sin and temptation, but He defeated the tempter. This is the reconciliation. Humanity itself had to win. The problem was with man, not with God! "For this reason he had to be made like his brothers [humanity] in every way, in order that he might . . . make atonement for the sins of the people" (Heb. 2:17).

Believing that Jesus entered the desert to be tempted in His *human* nature does not detract from His victory; it sweetens it. "For we do not have a high priest who is unable to sympathize with our [human] weakness, but we have one who has been tempted in every way, just as we are—yet was without sin" (Heb. 4:15).

How was God's Spirit added to Christ's human nature? The Bible states that Christ received power from God the Father, filling Him with the Holy Ghost. Human nature alone cannot win! Adam proved that. Christ went out, empowered by God Himself: "And the Holy Spirit descended on him in a bodily form like a dove" (Luke 3:22). The Bible tells us that "Jesus, full of the Holy Spirit, . . . was led by the Spirit in the desert, where for forty days he was tempted by the devil" (Luke 4:1). We have His Spirit too when we have Jesus.

In the Old Testament, God foretold the humanity of Christ being augmented by the Spirit to make Him righteous and faithful: "And there shall come forth a rod out of the stem of Jesse [humanity], and a Branch shall grow out of his roots: And the spirit of the Lord shall rest upon him, . . . And righteousness shall be the girdle of his loins, and faithfulness the girdle of his reins" (Isa. 11:1, 5, KJV). The Holy Spirit empowered and transformed the humanity of the second Adam into victory for us that continues today through the same power. Who gives it? Jesus, baptizing us with the Holy Spirit (Luke 3:16), accomplishes the same victory in our lives today if we commit ourselves. We will examine the outpouring, the baptism, and the filling of the Holy Spirit in chapters 6 and 8.

In trying to appreciate the humanity of Christ, we return once more to a balanced perspective. Jesus Christ is also God. The devil himself confessed that Jesus, the human who stood before him, was divine. "You are the Son of God" (Mark 3:11; see also Mark 5:7; Luke 4:41; Acts 19:15). Peter also testified to Christ's divine nature (Matt. 16:16);

the centurion at the foot of the cross said, "Surely this man was the Son of God" (Mark 15:39); Nathanael explained, "You are the Son of God; you are the King of Israel" (John 1:49). The Samaritans (John 4:42), Martha (John 11:27), and Thomas confessed the same truth (John 20:28). In all four Gospels, He is called "the Son of God," but He called Himself the Son of man . . . our friend!

That's an exciting revelation. Jesus Christ (God) became man and gave us total victory over man's sin, death, and eternal punishment. We can identify with Him completely and expect others to do so as we tell them about His saving grace. Surely, in order for us to be effective, we must present the second Adam, Jesus of Nazareth, through the authority and enablement of the Holy Spirit. However, we may not expect an acceptance of the witness without God's gift of faith. "For by grace are ye saved through faith" (Eph. 2:8, KJV). Do we understand faith well enough to recognize it as a vital complex force in our lives? We said earlier that we cannot share our faith. Why? What is faith?

5

Faith

Faith means many things to many people. We must be careful that those with whom we share the gospel possess a clear knowledge of *saving* faith. The Bible tells us that "faith is being sure of what we hope for and certain of what we do not see" (Heb. 11:1). Faith, a gift from God, will be an active, growing principle within every genuine Christian. In our scientific age, so much misunderstanding exists about faith that skilled witnessing requires careful presentation of this core truth.

Our faith is supposed to "move mountains," but often we can't even stir a molehill because *historic* faith is confused with, or substituted for, *saving* faith. I'm not referring to those without faith, those who deny the existence of God. My concern centers on anyone who agrees that Jesus Christ existed, came to earth, lives co-eternally with the Father, was born of a virgin, suffered and died on the cross, rose again the third day, and ascended to heaven.

None of this means anything to us if it remains just a series of historical facts, and facts they are. Even the devil believes this (James 2:19). Facts by themselves only constitute a record of events. When we translate such facts into a vital, everyday relationship with Christ, we have saving faith. Although both kinds of faith, saving and historical, are directed toward Jesus Christ, the first reaps eternal benefits, and the latter only expresses an academic conclusion.

I talked once with a grown man I'd known since the day he was born. He had his "faith" wrapped up in six words, "whoever believes . . . [shall] have everlasting life" (John 3:16). He added seven words of testimony: "I believe in Jesus; therefore, I'm saved." I have no doubt, today, about his real salvation, but there's a lot more behind the word *believe* than he was willing to recognize at that point. Historical faith is dormant, static, dead, and cold. It requires only mental assent.

Saving faith, on the other hand, produces action arising from an overt commitment fed through a heartfelt trust. Saving faith becomes so much a part of one's subjective self that it is often recognized as an avalanche or vocation of good works. Saving faith lives vibrantly and vitally, without serious doubt or challenge. Saving faith is the matrix around which God's grace—salvation in Jesus Christ—is rooted. Saving faith, a gift, rearranges one's priorities in life. What this really means is that in witnessing we need not insist on "giving up" this or that. After conversion, all things become new, including our priorities, but saving faith involves even more, and the Scriptures give us a working definition.

A Biblical Explanation

Saving faith is salvation	Whoever believes and is baptized will be saved (Mark 16:16).
in Jesus Christ	Salvation is found in no one else; for there is no other name under heaven given to men by which we must be saved (Acts 4:12).

who gives us an access to grace	Therefore, just as sin entered the world through one man, and death through sin, . . . to all men, . . . how much more did God's grace and the gift that came by the grace of the one man, Jesus Christ, overflow to the many (Rom. 5:12, 15).
by dying on the cross,	For God so loved the world that he gave his one and only Son (John 3:16).
by fulfilling the law and God's promise,	Through faith and patience [we] inherit what has been promised [of God to Abraham] (Heb. 6:12).
and by giving us his Holy Spirit,	Through Christ Jesus, so that by faith we might receive the promise of the Spirit (Gal. 3:14).
who for the sake of our righteousness	We have been saying that Abraham's faith was credited to him as righteousness (Rom. 4:9).
made us to be sons of God through the blessings given Abraham,	Understand, then, that those who believe are children of Abraham (Gal. 3:6).
with power to heal	Is any one of you sick? He should call the elders of the church to pray over him and anoint him with oil in the name of the Lord. And the prayer offered in faith will make the sick person well (James 5:14–15).

and to witness unto eternal life,	Whoever hears my word and believes him who sent me has eternal life (John 5:24).
expecting that eternal life starting right now	He who believes has everlasting life (John 6:47).
as an answer to prayer.	"Have faith in God," Jesus answered. "I tell you the truth, . . . whatever you ask for in prayer, believe that you will receive it, and it will be yours" (Mark 11: 22–24).

In other words, faith is a recognition of the implantation (ingrafting) of His personality (or Spirit) into ours. That is the biblical explanation of saving faith and the core of our message, but faith has many dimensions that must be fully understood and communicated. In the language of a chemist, *saving faith* would be a complex compound made up of elements such as action, experience, trust, dependence, obedience, prayer, election, power, surrender, and witnessing—mixed together with human responsibility.

Action

Suppose you and I are up in a light plane at about ten thousand feet and the engine stops! We are out of gas. There is nowhere to land safely; so we trim the ship, pull the flaps down, and hope our rate of descent is a slow glide. Two parachutes are on board, but only you know how to jump. We both put on our parachutes, and you instruct me on how to pull the rip cord. You tell me that after I jump and pull the cord the parachute *will* open. I would probably believe you because you are living proof that it has opened every time for you so far, but that's only historic faith. Until I actually jumped out of the plane, I would not be demonstrating or validating saving faith. Action validates God's saving faith.

James was strong on this point. He said, "Faith by itself, if it is not accompanied by action, is dead" (James 2:17); and again, "As the body without the spirit is dead, so faith without deeds is dead" (James 2:26); and of course, the text everyone knows: "Be ye doers of the word, and not hearers only" (James 1:22, KJV). Only if we jump obediently into the Christian life, as out of an airplane, do we demonstrate saving faith.

The opposite of action would probably be doubt and inaction. Jesus rebuked doubting in general (Matt. 14:31) and specifically drew our attention to the matter: "If . . . God clothes the grass of the field, which is here today and tomorrow is thrown into the fire, will he not much more clothe you, O you of little faith?" (Matt. 6:30).

Experience

Consider an infant, less than two years old, jumping off the dining room table into your outstretched arms. When you first placed him up there in an established and stable position, you probably had to coax him with many reassuring words and gestures before he would entrust himself to you and actually leap off the table into your arms. But after jumping once or twice, the child established "saving faith" through experience. Now you can hardly get him back up onto the table before he is already in the air. When it becomes obvious that this faith is too questionless or based too much on experience and not enough on the other elements necessary for good balance, then we—as wise parents—call a halt to the fun for a later time.

Experience "breeds" faith, but it adds only one more element to the development of the whole and does not eliminate other aspects. It lends itself to the realization of *trust*.

Trust

Through the experience of being caught safely each time, the infant unlocked and brought into play the element of trust. Saving faith is trust as Solomon seems to say in Proverbs: "Trust in the Lord with all thine heart; and lean not unto thine own understanding" (Prov. 3:5, KJV). Saving faith does not limit itself to salvation but extends into every facet of our relationship to Jesus. We trust Him to supply not only our eternal needs but our everyday needs as well. "Therefore [Jesus said] I tell you, do not worry about your life, what you will eat or drink; or about your body, what you will wear. Is not life [eternal] more important than food, and the body more important than clothes?" (Matt. 6:25).

Don't be embarrassed to emphasize that Jesus knows all about our bodies since He had a body just like ours. With His experience we can trust Him to know what is best in every sphere of life—both for body and for soul. Actually, we should have no problem trusting someone who has already traveled where He is leading us, who has already run the course that we are running (Eph. 4:8–10). Our only problem is that our spirit must step down before His Spirit will step up!

The Faith Metaphor

We live in the space age; so picture with me the vastness of outer space. You and I are traveling along through space. We (our bodies) are space capsules enroute to somewhere, either heaven or the outer darkness of hell. The trip itself is the span of time we call life.

We individually require fuel to propel us through space. The fuel is prayer. There are two kinds of prayer: prayer to God the Father through Jesus Christ (superior fuel) and prayer to myself or someone else (inferior fuel).

Two kinds of ignition systems are available: the standard equipment system (inferior because it is sparked by the fiery darts of the evil one) and the Christian system (superior because it is sparked by the flame of the Holy Spirit). Fuel, by itself, will not move us. It must be ignited to produce thrust, which in our metaphor is *faith*. The thrust, or faith, that comes from inferior fuel (self-prayer, self-hope, self-sufficiency) combined with the inferior ignition system of the devil (his fiery darts, lies, and ploys) is insufficient to free us from our earthly orbit. We would just circle around and finally become lost in space forever. Similarly, we would fail to measure up to God's standards or fail to witness for Him through our own personalities and abilities, apart from the ingrafting of the Holy Spirit.

Therefore, the thrust (faith) which is produced from superior fuel (real Christ-centered prayer) coupled to a superior ignition system (the flame of the Holy Spirit) produces thrust (saving faith) that propels us from our worldly orbit to heaven. The interaction of the Holy Spirit and real prayer to God is *within* us (within the capsule). Our faith (thrust) is outside us. Faith of itself, or thrust in itself, cannot be seen; only the effects are noticeable. Either the capsule is flying a straight and narrow path with solid thrust (faith), or it travels erratically with insufficient thrust, or faith.

Thrust with no direction is useless; so all capsules need a navigator. We are either our own navigators, or Jesus, who claimed to be the Way of Life, becomes ingrafted into our "capsules" as Navigator. So we have two choices: We can either try to make it on our own—remaining our own pilots —or we can appropriate Jesus Christ as substitute Navigator, stepping down so that He can step up.

Component Parts

The *capsule* itself is you. *Superior fuel* is Christian prayer in the true sense. *Inferior fuel* is self-prayer. It is not prayed in Christ's name but is uttered solely in one's own strength. The *standard ignition system* is sparked by the fiery darts of the devil, and the *superior ignition system* is sparked by the flame of the Holy Spirit. *Ground Control* is God the Father in heaven who is the same for everyone. The *standard navigator* is self, the same for everyone at the outset *Special Navigator* is Jesus Christ, exchanged for self at no charge. (This is not an "automatic pilot." No "lock-in" is available.) *Thrust* is faith. It can be either saving or historic, depending on the kind of fuel and ignition system used. *Contrail* (the white streak from a jet) is one's personal witness. *Many contrails* seen together in a straight and narrow trajectory compose the visible church. The *homing beacon* is located in heaven. It beams its signal in 360 degrees, but a special receiver is required to pick it up. The *pretuned receiver*, located far behind the instrument panel, is a special piece of equipment found in only a few capsules. It is capable of receiving God's homing beacon from anywhere in space. It is placed in some capsules from eternity but not discovered until later in life. The *flight* plan, or trajectory, is the holy, infallible Scripture. *Distance traveled* is measured by the level of individual sanctification attained, and *course corrections* are tribulations. *Proper sequence* of all these events is God's grace. *Holds* are our free will to procrastinate.

Obedience

Saving faith, or thrust, is capable of propelling us to heaven! It consists of much prayer sparked by the Holy Spirit. Out in the vastness of space, heaven is not easy to find. The flight plan—God's Word—is not only narrow and straight but also difficult to apply for both new and mature Christians. Therefore, in this long space shot of life, there will have to be frequent course corrections. Obviously, the data necessary to perform a course correction accurately is of no value unless the element of obedience is brought into focus. Without obedience, faith wavers and precludes its validity. We must constantly prove our faith by continuing in obedience through many course corrections.

If our faith wavers, our only hope is a course correction, a new burst of faith made possible through serious prayer and the spark of the Holy Spirit. The burst (also called a burn) is preceded by a calculated countdown. Do not marvel that a reburn is necessary. True to our sinful stubbornness, some Christians will always refuse to obey or correct immediately; instead, they call for a halt in the countdown. When they do this—and they can because of their free will—God may send tribulations, pressures, and crises until a perfect obedience emerges.

Our Lord has promised His elect that "he who began a
good work in you will carry it on to completion until the day
of Christ Jesus" (Phil. 1:6). The course correction will
occur, it's only a matter of how much tribulation will be
necessary to bring it about and how much stalling the Christian wants to engage in first.

Prayer

Prayer (fuel) is a pure element in itself and comes as a
direct gift from our Lord who made it available when He
became our Mediator. "No one comes to the Father except
through me" (John 14:6), Jesus said. And no one will ever
fly to heaven, or find the Father, except through Jesus the
Navigator, who gives us prayer-fuel in the first place.
Therefore, prayer is one more element of saving faith. It is
also a real fuel in life. According to James, prayer and faith
are inseparable. "If any of you lacks wisdom, he should ask
God [prayer], who gives generously to all without finding
fault, and it will be given to him. But when he asks, he must
believe [faith] and not doubt, because he who doubts is like
a wave of the sea, blown and tossed by the wind" (James
1:5–6).

The force of prayer which is capable of producing an unwavering faith is not always fully appropriated by inquirers
or even by new converts. In such cases, our Navigator (Jesus
Christ) makes intercession with the Father. Paul said this
about our Lord: "Therefore he is able to save completely
those who come to God through him, because he always
lives to intercede for them" (Heb. 7:25). Jesus told us
plainly that He prayed for Simon Peter: "But I have prayed
for you, Simon, that your faith may not fail. And when you

have returned to me, strengthen your brothers" (Luke 22:32).

The point is this: Those who are lost in space and who seek the only Way through the only true Navigator may not be fully aware of how to pray, and therefore they are unable to recognize the thrust and trust they require. Thank God that they are aided by a loving, interceding Savior into that awareness and knowledge.

Witness

The thrust of a jet produces a contrail through the sky which is visible for miles. In our metaphor a contrail is the witness one produces. Each capsule, regardless of the fuel or spark used, is producing a contrail; and every person alive is witnessing either for or against our Lord. Jesus said: "He who is not with me is against me, and he who does not gather with me, scatters" (Luke 11:23). No one, therefore, can be neutral.

The witness contrail is the result of the thrust of one's faith, and it is either broad or narrow, straight or erratic. Christians can produce either; non-Christians can only produce the broad and erratic contrail. Everyone is witnessing something! By their contrails, you shall know them.

Dependence

With the elements of saving faith present (prayer and the Holy Spirit mixed according to grace), a saving thrust is produced that propels us forward according to our flight plan (God's Word). Dependence upon God's Word is another essential element of saving faith. Mile by mile His Word assures us that we are on course and will arrive safely home. Paul said, "Faith comes from hearing the . . . word of Christ" (Rom. 10:17).

The dependence element of saving faith must also come into play in darkness when we first realize that we have drifted and need a course correction. Dependence on God, an evidence of surrender, keeps us from calling for a halt in the countdown. Each element interacts with the others (subject to God's grace) and finally produces the compound of saving faith. We have a responsibility not to stifle our faith in Christ by considering ourselves self-sufficient.

Election

Picture with me a space capsule enjoying its own pleasure and following its own course—lost in space. Being earthbound, it is hopelessly circling the planet without purpose. The contrail or witness is wavering, broad, and sporadic to the point where the observer would never identify this capsule as one of the elect, yet it might be. None of us has any way of knowing. Only after the election has been activated, or validated, can we identify the elect by their fruits, their contrails.

Before anyone can turn on to Jesus as Navigator, he or she must first activate a receiver supplied as standard equipment by the Manufacturer (God) to only the elect. This (election) receiver is so sophisticated that it has baffled theologians for ages. The most frustrating thing about it is that, prior to its activation, there is absolutely no way of telling who has this receiver and who hasn't.

But by contrails we know who has and has not yet produced a saving faith. It now becomes the obligation of every Christian—new and matured—to bring those who are lost into a saving faith so that they too will be able to fly to heaven. We are justified by a saving faith, "according to his eternal purpose which he accomplished in Christ Jesus our [Navigator] Lord" (Eph. 3:11).

I do not desire to present an apology here for election as a scriptural doctrine; however, if you are interested in finding a few New Testament verses that describe God's people as the elect, look up Matthew 24:22, Luke 18:7, Romans 8:33, 2 Timothy 2:10, and 1 Peter 1:2. In general, throughout Scripture God's people are identified as a peculiar people, a peculiar treasure (Exod. 19:5), chosen by Jehovah (Deut. 14:2), exalted above all nations (Deut. 26:19; 1 Sam. 12:22), and prepared for "in-flight service" to fly to heaven (Luke 1:17; Acts 15:14).

The Power Potential

In the words of our metaphor, thrust (faith) is the power that propels us through space; however, the only power that is allowed to be expended along the flight path toward heaven is that power strong enough to produce an unwavering contrail (witness). This thrust drives us into the holy Word of God which is the flight plan for our lives. With such thrust we are moved forward, advancing into the Word and uncovering God's will from it—ground control. Paul said, "With this in mind, we constantly pray for you, that our God may count you worthy of his calling, and that by his power he may fulfill every good purpose of yours and every act prompted by your faith" (2 Thess. 1:11). When we lose this power, we lose our heading and will become lost in space or, at best, drift off course.

Remember that we always maintain a power of sorts. When we operate on our own, ignited by the fiery darts of Satan and self-prayer, we produce faith that is not saving in its thrust. "Not everyone has [saving] faith" (2 Thess. 3:2), Paul warns! Jesus also warns of this loss of power-thrust-faith: "That your faith may not *fail*" (Luke 22:32)! Inadequate (nonsaving) faith produces erratic and offensive contrails, or witnesses.

Human Responsibility

Those Christians and non-Christians who refuse to abide in Jesus Christ, who refuse to accept Him as their personal Navigator, become a menace to navigation. God warned us: "Hold unswervingly to the hope we profess, . . . [without wavering and] not give up meeting together" (Heb. 10:23, 25). "Meeting together" is the conglomerate of many contrails along the straight and narrow path involved in what we call the visible church. Those who operate with a lack of sufficient thrust will never overcome the pull of the world. John told us that "everyone born of God has overcome the world. This is the victory that has overcome the world, even our faith" (1 John 5:4).

Not all who fly the course in the visible church stay there. Jesus spoke of such possible failures: "They believe for a while, but in the time of testing they fall away" (Luke 8:13); and Paul said, "Some have rejected these and so have shipwrecked their faith" (1 Tim. 1:19).

The phenomenon of self-destruction—shipwreck—indicates our human responsibility. Paul warned: "Study [Scripture] to shew thyself approved unto God . . . [lest you] . . . overthrow [or destroy] the faith of some. Nevertheless . . . the Lord knoweth them that are his" (2 Tim. 2:15, 18–19, KJV). Besides shipwrecking ourselves, we may even wreck the faith of others because we don't always turn from our wicked ways. This is the picture of many Christian lives: one conflict after another, one failure after another. One wonders why we don't measure up if we are truly new creatures in Christ. There is a double-sided answer to that question. When we fail, it's because we've given "audience" to the devil, and when we do that, we grieve the Holy Spirit. Christ mortally wounded the devil. He didn't do away with him; so evil is still present. This is just a fact of life with the Christian and part of the reason we don't always measure up. The other reason is that we too often neglect the Holy Spirit's function in our lives; we tend to confuse the entire issue surrounding the Holy Spirit's outpouring, baptism, and filling. This lack of understanding His Spirit and repeated failures in measuring up present a real problem and challenge to Christians in their witness. God warns us that "everyone who confesses the name of the Lord must turn away from wickedness" (2 Tim. 2:19)! How? Only through an understanding of both powers—the outpouring, baptism, the filling of Christ's Spirit, and the devil's tricks.

6

The Outpouring, the Baptism, and the Filling of Christ's Holy Spirit

In our witness we are sure to run into terminology surrounding the outpouring, baptism, and filling of the Holy Spirit. These terms confuse most of us and frequently create massive controversies, splitting churches and setting husband against wife, family against family, and friend against friend.

What an effective ploy of the devil to control all he can of individual commitment before that commitment grows into a deeper, more wonderful knowledge and victory. With the new convert, for instance, the devil might try to obstruct any deepening of the new loyalty to Jesus Christ. He can do this in many ways, but two are his favorites. He may try to involve new Christians in a search for an anointing, thus confusing them about the baptism or the filling of the Holy Spirit. He may simply strive to deceive new Christians by suggesting that they ignore the entire subject of the Holy Spirit. All of this he seeks to accomplish on an individual basis, mimicking the God who deals with each of us in our distinctive personalities as separate entities.

Every Christian must be aware that being filled with the

Holy Spirit is not the same as being baptized by the Holy Spirit and that both of these phenomena are two thousand years removed from the outpouring of the Holy Spirit. Nowhere in Scripture do we read anything about a special sensation that some would like us to believe accompanies these three events.

Therefore, the starting point in discussing the Holy Spirit in our witness must always be the recognition that the outpouring took place at Pentecost, that the baptism occurs at the moment of each individual's personal conversion, and that the filling can and should be simultaneous with the baptism, even though it often follows many years later.

Every converted Christian has been baptized by the Holy Spirit! A few still remain confused enough to continue to seek the baptism later on. When one accepts Jesus Christ (conversion), he or she accepts the total Person of Christ, including His Spirit (the Holy Spirit). Paul stated it most emphatically: "You [who are in Christ Jesus (v. 1)], however, are controlled . . . by the Spirit, if the Spirit of God lives in you. And if anyone does not have the Spirit of Christ, he does not belong to Christ" (Rom. 8:9). Without the baptism of the Holy Spirit, Christ wouldn't be in us.

Paul told us that if we do not have the Spirit of Christ we "do not belong to Christ"; therefore, we aren't Christians. This is exactly why we encounter so many misunderstandings about possessing the Spirit. We confuse baptism with possessing one or two manifestations of the gift of the Spirit. Add to this the ever-increasing bewilderment surrounding the basic distinction between the Spirit's outpouring, baptism, and filling, and we've got good reason to sit down immediately and search the Scriptures.

When we accepted Jesus Christ, we received His Spirit; that's the baptism of the Holy Spirit. As born again Christians, we already have it. God said, "I will put my spirit within you, and cause you to walk in my statutes, and ye shall keep my judgments, and do them" (Ezek. 36:27, KJV). We have the same Spirit of God, the same Power, the same Guide abiding in our hearts that Ezekiel, Balaam (Num. 24:2), the seventy elders (Num. 11:25), Gideon (Judg. 6:43), Samson (Judg. 14:6), Saul (1 Sam. 10:10), David (1 Sam. 16:13), Simeon (Luke 2:25), and others had guiding them!

Let's first become aware of the presence of the Holy Spirit made possible through the outpouring of Jesus' Spirit two thousand years ago at Pentecost. In the Book of Acts we read, "God has raised this Jesus to life, and we [Luke and the disciples] are all witnesses of the fact" (Acts 2:32). Luke reminds us that he *saw* all of this. In verse 33, he goes on to tell us that Jesus is now "exalted to the right hand of God, he has received from the Father the promised Holy Spirit, and has poured out what you now see and hear."

This is probably one of the most electrifying verses of Scripture! The words "we are all witnesses to the fact" link what Luke saw with what Jesus did physically and with the fact that Jesus is now exalted in heaven. This is the same Jesus that Luke talked to, touched, and looked upon with his very eyes. Luke declares that this same Jesus is now not only exalted but has "received from the Father the promised Holy Spirit." What happened then? Pentecost! He *has* poured forth His Holy Spirit. Luke is telling us that the result of Jesus' exaltation is that "which ye now see and hear" (Acts 2:33, KJV)—the outpouring of the Holy Spirit.

The entire basis for the Holy Spirit's outpouring was Jesus Christ's exaltation. Do you realize what this is not saying? It labels as ridiculous all notions that we must do something in order to receive the outpouring of the Spirit. We don't have to do anything. The Holy Spirit was poured out because Jesus was exalted, not because of you or me. The outpouring had absolutely no relationship to any of man's merits, only to the merits of Jesus Christ. Because of His merits, He was exalted. Because of God's plan of substitutionary salvation, His merits become ours and we are exalted!

This is the same pattern, the same logic, that God uses all through His plan of salvation. Because Jesus shed His blood on the cross, we received forgiveness from our sins, not because of us. Because of Jesus' resurrection we receive a new victorious life, not because of us. Because of Jesus' exaltation there was an outpouring of His Holy Spirit on Pentecost, not because of us.

Remission of our sins came from the cross, regeneration, from the resurrection, and the outpouring, from the exaltation. It's all because of Him. Praise God for Jesus!

It must be sickeningly humorous to God to hear some tell others to wait for a manifestation of the Holy Spirit two thousand years after the fact, or to claim some merit for receiving what Christ already earned. The Holy Spirit is a gift. The Holy Spirit is God, the third Person of the Trinity, made manifest by the virtue of Christ Jesus sitting at the right hand of God the Father in heaven. The outpouring of this gift, therefore, is unconditional.

The baptism of the Holy Spirit is also unconditional in the strictest sense of the word. We *do* have to make a choice to accept Jesus before conversion is complete; however, the unconditional aspect of the baptism of the Holy Spirit (at the time of conversion) is the fact that the very conversion *contains* the baptism. "If anyone does not have the Spirit . . . he does not belong to Christ" (Rom. 8:9). The Holy Spirit confirms that each of us is God's child in Christ (Rom.

8:16). Paul put it this way: "Those who are led by the Spirit of God [they] are sons of God . . . you received the Spirit [of adoption] who makes you sons. And by him we cry, '*Abba*, Father'" (Rom. 8:14, 15).

The *filling* of the Spirit, however is not unconditional; it is contingent. It is conditioned upon our free will as it interacts with our faith constantly to attend and monitor the fullness. Our will to be filled depends upon our faith or lack of doubt. One way to rid ourselves of doubt is to increase the element of awareness. In this case, the object of our awareness would be the Holy Spirit's presence in our hearts since the day of our conversion.

So then, how can each of us, as Christians, become more aware of the Holy Spirit in our hearts? First, we must recognize some of the things the Holy Spirit has been doing in our lives and in the hearts of Christians all these years. Every time we prayed, we did it because the Spirit moved us (Rom. 8:26; Eph. 6:18). Every time we sin, we are called to repent by the Holy Spirit in our hearts (Ezek. 36:27; John 14:17; 1 Cor. 3:16). He is focusing guilt upon our sins (John 16:8) and thus calling us to the confession of 1 John 1:9. He's the "still, small voice" within who warns us, directs us, and wants to control us (1 John 2:27). He's been there since we first believed.

The baptism of the Holy Spirit is a personal matter and happens in one heart at a time. Because we are baptized by the Holy Spirit the moment we accept Jesus Christ as Savior, we must admit our awareness that He is within.

When God blesses our witness and people pray to receive Christ, they don't pray in the hope that Jesus will die on the cross to forgive them! They pray with thanksgiving because Jesus Christ has already been crucified and has already paid the price by shedding his blood. Jesus isn't going to become Lord, He *is* Lord already (Acts 2:36, 5:31; Rom. 10:9; 1 Cor. 1:9, 12:3; Eph. 4:5; Tit. 6:15; Rev. 1:5, 19:16).

Just as salvation (the baptism of the Holy Spirit) is an individual happening, the filling of the Holy Spirit is an individual event. He's been poured out unconditionally, and He's in the heart of every believer unconditionally; but each believer must surrender or yield in order to be filled. The filling is predicated upon our free will to become aware, surrender, repent, and appropriate His Spirit.

God, in His excellent wisdom and total sovereignty, has ordained that our free will can grieve the Holy Spirit (Eph. 4:30), and we can quench the Holy Spirit (1 Thess. 5:19). Is this what we want? Or do we desire to be filled now that we've been baptized by the Holy Spirit the day we accepted Christ?

When we are filled with the Holy Spirit, we'll know it. God's dealings with us are always personal. The new convert may say, "But if I'll know it, why don't I . . .?" There's only one answer to that question, and it is universal: because we have not yet met the conditions for being filled. If we are born again, He's there. The next step is to stop ignoring Him and become aware of Him. For Jesus' sake, Christians must also stop denying Him by claiming that all this "Holy Spirit business" belongs to the first century. Oh, how that must grieve God who has promised the Holy Spirit to them and to their seed (Isa. 59:21) through the exaltation of Jesus Christ.

Besides ignoring Him and denying Him, many Christians too often condemn special gifts that His Spirit provides— one of which is speaking in tongues. We should not condemn the Holy Spirit for giving this gift to some, let alone condemn those to whom He has given this particular gift.

Too many Christians today expect some sort of super-natural sign when they are baptized or filled with the Holy Spirit; and far too many Christians expect this to be limited to the most controversial manifestation of all—speaking in tongues. How ridiculous to try to limit God to one mode of expression when we know that He has seen fit to give everyone a different and distinct personality.

The Holy Spirit is that Force within that modifies us in ourselves yet allows us to be ourselves. This freedom (called free will) can be focused, instead, for evil, and that's when we fail to measure up to God's commands to each of us collectively and individually. Surely, as we witness to others, some will look at our imperfections (because we are still sinners) and wonder why we don't always measure up. Why don't we?

7
Why We Don't Always Measure Up

Have you ever tossed something into a puddle just to gain some insidious satisfaction from distorting the surface of the water? The devil does this to us everyday. When it happens, any reflection of Christ's rainbow of love in us is completely perverted. Humanly speaking, this could destroy our witness for Christ.

Conflicts in the Christian life are nothing new. Throughout the years, the devil has craftily initiated all kinds of misunderstandings. Many of these surround basic doctrinal issues—aside from those we've just studied—such as individual forgiveness and rules for Christian living. These quandaries have created some serious misrepresentations of Scripture's purest teachings.

God's Holy Spirit in Christ and the evil spirit are in direct conflict, and the battleground is our spirit. There's a war going on in each of us. We can best prepare for this battle by developing within ourselves a deeper awareness of the enemy's methods. This chapter is on the devil. Its purpose is to place ourselves in a victorious position. Jesus Christ came to earth and mortally wounded our enemy; yet our foe is still busy tricking us into failure. Whenever we witness, we should expect all kinds of harassment from the devil. The more we understand about him, the more potent and alert our communication of the gospel can be. How does he operate? Evil spirits exist all around us in many forms. Most appear very desirable and seem to assure gratification. We are not possessed by evil spirits or their forms, just obsessed by them. Their strength far exceeds your and my ability to subdue them. We are totally helpless when confronted alone, and if that were the end of the story, we would be eternally lost.

Thank God, it's only part of the story. Our hope—our only hope with our inferior spirits—is the superior Spirit of God through Jesus Christ who has already permanently handicapped the devil and all his forces. Apart from His Spirit, however, there is no victory from evil obsessions. New Christians—even mature Christians—don't always realize this. Evil spirits are the most underrated power in the world today!

The Devil Made Me Do It

Evil spirits are so crafty and cunning, even pleasant at times, that we allow them to fool us into sin. The devil even supplies excuses for sin, prompting us to *excuse ourselves* rather than seek God's forgiveness. One such excuse is a popular quip that many people consider cute: "The devil made me do it." Many of us have probably smiled at this lie.

Evil spirits do not make us sin. If they did, they would be responsible for human immorality instead of you or me. God holds us personally accountable for our sins. He will judge us, not the devil. "The devil made me do it" is probably one of the most destructive heresies Satan has going for himself today. It is a sinister tactic resulting in an extremely dangerous attack on the core of truth. We must recognize it as a falsehood and total impossibility, not just an innocent joke.

How do we know this? Jesus Christ, being "led by the Spirit" (Matt. 4:1), went out into the desert to show us that the devil doesn't make us do anything. Jesus showed us how to handle temptation. The way of deliverance has always been the Holy Scriptures. Every time the devil tempted our Lord, He answered from Scripture until the devil began quoting Scripture to Jesus in yet another attempt to make Him sin (Matt. 4:6).

Evil Spirits Use Christians

Evil spirits don't merely use quips, they use us. Christians often do the devil's bidding without even realizing it. Often we begin to do something "for the Lord," only to end up crediting it to the devil's account and to his delight. Peter is a good example of this. Jesus had told His disciples that "where I am going, you cannot follow" (John 13:36). Peter, not understanding what the Lord was saying about His death, resurrection, and ascension, boldly stated that he would lay his life down for his Lord (verse 37). Jesus forewarned Peter that "before the rooster crows, you will disown me three times!" (John 13:38). Peter did. First, when the girl at the door of the high priest's courtyard asked him if he was another of Christ's disciples, Peter replied, "I am not" (John 18:17b), as he stood warming himself by the fire with Christ's enemies.

Peter denied Jesus twice more (verses 25 and 27) "and at

that moment a rooster began to crow" (verse 27). The crow-ing, to others, was of no significance; but to Peter it had to be like the voice of God reminding him that he had failed his Lord three times over, crediting the failures to the devil!

If we were completely honest with ourselves, we would have to admit that we, too, probably try to accomplish things alone (without God), only to have the devil win be-cause we refuse to resist him.

Early Christians had similar problems, and James became firm with them. He said, "Submit yourselves, then, to God. Resist the devil, and he will flee from you. Come near to God and he will come near to you. Wash your hands, you sinners, and purify your hearts, you double-minded" (James 4:7–8). On the other hand, we shouldn't expect perfection in this life. Instead, we should claim Christ's perfection as ours and then enjoy His victory over His (and our) defeated foe—the devil!

Evil spirits have still another way of confusing the thoughts and reasoning power of the Christian. If the slogan "The devil made me do it" doesn't work, he has another shibboleth that might: "God made me do it."

God Made Me Do It

The devil has a lot of fun by mixing this one with the doctrines of predestination, God's sovereignty, and human responsibility. Who is responsible? Did God plan Adam's fall with the full knowledge of His plan of redemption? Did God make Adam do it? Often, those who would like to argue these points do so to avoid learning more about the Person of Jesus Christ. By changing the subject, they can shun the invitation to grow in the Lord.

Although God did foreknow Adam's sin and the sins we have committed and will commit, this does not make Him the author of sin. In His infinite knowledge, our Lord is free to plan around the sins already performed and to overrule them for our benefit because "we know that in all things God works for the good of those who love him, who have been called according to his purpose" (Rom. 8:28). God never authors sin. "When tempted, no one should say, 'God is tempting me'" (James 1:13). God did not make us do it, but now that we've done it, He has a perfect right to turn it to our profit if He so chooses and if we repent.

We have no way of knowing which of our sins God might use, if any (Isa. 55:8–9). We are duty bound (Isa. 55:7), therefore, by the law of human responsibility to conquer every sin, everywhere, every time (Rom. 6:23). When we fail, and we will (Rom. 7), it is because we are weak. Only after the fact can God use our sins to reprove those whom He loves and knew from the very beginning (Eph. 1:11, 1 Pet. 1:12–22; Heb. 6:17–20; Acts 13:28).

That God does not author sin is the only conclusion we can come to after reading His holy Word. To assume otherwise is to proclaim another falsehood of the evil one. Earlier I quoted the first part of a text, saving the last part until now: "When tempted, no one should say, 'God is tempting me.' For God cannot be tempted by evil, nor does he tempt anyone" (James 1:13).

"Oh, the depth . . . of God!
   How unsearchable his judgments,
   and his paths beyond tracing out."
                              Rom. 11:33

Spirits in Conflict with the Doctrines

Evil spirits also enjoy working in the hearts of Christians, confusing them into misusing or abusing pure doctrines of Scripture. The devil wouldn't be so bold as to question openly the validity of a doctrine to some believer; however, he may twist truth to the eternal detriment of the believer by having him place his eternal hope in the doctrine rather than in the Person of Jesus Christ. Confused Christians often hang on to the false security found in doctrinal structure at the expense of a personal faith in the Savior. It's the same old conflict between historic and saving faith—believing Him as opposed to believing *in* Him. Doctrines are for our edification; Jesus Christ is our only means of salvation.

When used out of context, God's purest truths become hollow dogmas and only raise additional questions and more false answers. Because of this, one should not introduce the doctrines of predestination in the initial stages of evangelism. It is purely academic at that point. Even with the mature Christian, the devil can effectively abuse this doctrine of election if one's hope rests in the teaching instead of in Christ. Hope in laws or propositions by themselves (whether used in initial stages of evangelism or not) frustrates the grace of God. Paul laid it out clearly: "I do not set aside the grace of God, for if righteousness could be gained through the law, Christ died for nothing" (Gal. 2:21)!

When evil spirits coerce one into relying on doctrines rather than upon Jesus, they offer a pseudofaith in a pseudosavior.

Evil Spirits in Conflict with the Church

Evil spirits also operate effectively in another area—the church. They use subtle ways. The devil would never ask you, or the new Christian, to forsake going to church—just fall asleep in it every week, or if that's too noticeable, drift off with your eyes open. The devil will comfort you with still another of his favorite catchwords: "There's safety in numbers." This is never a true statement when the subject is salvation! God deals with us individually.

There is no safety in numbers with Jesus Christ. Jesus talked about that once: "Those eighteen who died when the tower in Siloam fell on them—do you think they were more guilty than all the others living in Jerusalem? I tell you, no! But unless you [everyone of you, individually] repent, you too will all perish" (Luke 13:4–5).

The basic question is not whether the church or the doctrines are true or even whether they are redemptive; the real issue is: Where do you stand in your individual relationship to the Person of Jesus Christ? That's the only important matter. "Examine yourselves to see whether you are in the faith; test yourselves . . . that Christ Jesus is in you" (2 Cor. 13:5). In other words, Paul warned us not to get all wrapped up in proving whether dogmas are good or bad, true or false; instead, we should examine ourselves first to be sure that Jesus lives in each of us.

Both the church and the doctrines are a part of growth in Christ. They promote sanctification, and they stimulate our edification, but they can never be substituted for salvation. "For there is no other name under heaven given to men by which we must be saved" (Acts 4:12) except the name of Jesus. Ultimately your witnessing must bring your contact down *that* road.

Spirits in Conflict with God's Forgiveness

Have you ever awakened from a very bad dream only to thank God that it was only a dream? Isn't that a great feeling? Such is the solace of forgiveness in Jesus Christ if we'd only allow Him to truly forgive us. One of the problem areas of the Christian life is that we either refuse to accept forgiveness or we accept it intellectually while still maintaining guilt feelings that rob us of the beautiful reprieve that comes from His full, complete, perfect, finished forgiveness.

Actually committing a sin is far worse than a bad dream. Soon guilt feelings begin to drift in like a heavy fog and envelop us until we enter other conflicts. Will God talk to us, using these guilt feelings to a point of immediate repentance, or will the devil dupe us, using these same guilt feelings and leave us totally frustrated? Feelings can be easily co-opted by the devil and should not be relied upon when facts are available. We are told to discover the joy of God's favor, not to dwell on the fear of His disapproval and punishment.

The devil can use feelings of guilt to his sinful advantage. He begins by convincing us that God must be very angry with us for our sin. How can we have the audacity to call ourselves Christian? How can we be such hypocrites? How can we say one thing and then do the opposite? How can we slap Jesus in the face? How can we turn our back on Him if we really love Him? These are real problems in the Christian's life. The devil will drive all hope from us if we allow him to, and he need not lie to us to confuse us either.

Jesus Became Sin for Us

The devil has a few other things going for him—thanks to us. For some reason we seem to want to paint a mental picture of Jesus dressed in white and unwilling to get dirty, especially if it means getting dirty because *we* come out of the filthy mire of our mud puddles. The fact is that sin doesn't "shock" Christ!

Jesus Christ came into this world *because* of sin, to forgive us for our sins. Our sins are gone, but sin (singular) continues. We must never allow the devil to divert us from the forgiveness of sins by drawing our attention to the vileness of sin. All the devil has to do is suggest that you and I are too sinful for our sinless Christ, and we will probably agree, forgetting that Jesus' entire mission upon this earth was to become sin for us.

Paul said it best: "God made him who had no sin to be sin for us, so that in him we might become the righteousness of God" (2 Cor. 5:21). Have you ever heard anything more shocking? God bankrupted Jesus in order to make us wealthy and worthy, to make us full of the righteousness of God Himself. What a fantastic exchange. This very one-sided affair is all to our favor and benefit. Praise God!

The terrible price Jesus had to pay to make us righteous makes us shudder to imagine that we, with our puny little minds, can even suggest that (in our righteousness) we might be "too sinful" for Jesus. How can we be suckered into these feelings of unworthiness unless we really don't believe that we *were* made the righteousness of God in the first place?

Pseudo-forgiveness

God's love is not spelled f-o-r-g-i-v-e-n-e-s-s. Love and forgiveness do not mean the same thing. Without true repentance, which includes a complete change of attitude toward each sin, there is no forgiveness. This is a promise from God (1 John 1:9).

Some books today state, in effect: "God loves everyone; He's forgiven everyone all of their sins—past, present, and future. He wants everyone to be free from guilt feelings. Be happy. Your sins are gone." Such statements lead us into more false securities and more feelings. They make God a bouncing bundle of love by completely ignoring His justice as it was brought to bear on our Lord and Savior Jesus Christ. They don't mention repentance or confession. God only promised forgiveness "*if* we confess our sins." Then "he is faithful and just and will forgive (1 John 1:9). When God gives us opportunity to discuss spiritual matters, remember to insist on the crucial importance of repentance and forgiveness.

The Conflict of New Sins

Conflicts in the Christian life continue. Jesus said, "Keep my commandments" (John 14:15, KJV). We agree we will; then we fall right on our face trying.

The devil will now play with our emotions even more by asking us how we could ever do such a thing. "Christians love Jesus," he says, "they don't hurt Him. You should question, therefore, whether or not you *are* a Christian." The devil might even point you to John 16:27 (he quoted Scriptures to Jesus while tempting Him, isn't it safe to assume he'd do that to us as well?) He'd ask you to explain how you can justify sinning and living in sin (Prov. 20:9), actually enjoying it (Tit. 3:3), and still ask for forgiveness again and again.

These aren't necessarily bad questions, except the devil's, trying to lead us down a dead-end street. He'll ask how we can pray for forgiveness in the holy name of Jesus when we just did something we *knew* was wrong. Soon we feel like hypocrites because he has us all wrapped up in guilt feelings. He manages capriciously to steal away Christ's blessed forgiveness promised to us in 1 John 1:9. Don't let him cloud up this promise.

No One Is Sent to Hell Because of His Sins

No one is judged or sent to hell because of his sins; each is condemned because of his unwillingness to repent and seek forgiveness for those sins. So grotesque, so fleshly, so fickle, so disastrous, so rotten are our sins (and their consequences) that we often become preoccupied with the sins rather than with forgiveness through repentance, confession, and prayer.

Conflicts in Multiplicity of Old Sins

When one repents and confesses each sin in search of God's forgiveness, he or she will receive it (1 John 1:9), but Satan will then be ready with the next conflict—the social, religious, economic, and even legal ramifications.

Seldom do we commit a sin that involves only ourselves. Usually there are others who have participated with us, either directly or indirectly, or know of our involvement. If the sin has social overtones, like "Watergate," there is the possibility that lies must be told to cover old lies. One lie leads to the next, and soon the sin compounds itself so far that the devil almost seems wisest when he suggests that we just throw in the towel and quit trying to be Christians! Don't let that happen to you or to the new Christian.

God said, "Evil men and impostors will go from bad to worse, deceiving and being deceived" (2 Tim. 3:13). The devil is adept at quoting Scripture too—out of context but also in context. He does this to his sinful advantage and to the Christian's disadvantage. Many passages in Scripture proclaim that we are sinners (Gen. 6:5; 1 Kings 8:46; Ps. 53:3; Rom. 3:32; 1 John 1:8, and others). Many passages also proclaim that we are sin*less* (Col. 1:28, 3:14; James 1:4; 2 Cor. 5:21; 1 Pet. 1:19, 2:22, and others). How can we be sinless sinners? At this point, many just give up. But listen to the secrets of God. We are sinless in Christ even though we are sinners in fact.

Now add another conflict: We are to *live* sinlessly in our sinful state right here and now in this life (Isa. 1:16; John 5:14; John 8:11; Rom. 6:12; 1 Cor. 15:34). The devil now has another hurdle for us to stumble over. How can we live sinlessly in a sinful state?

The devil says that the only logical conclusion is that we are either terrible sinners, awful hypocrites, or extremely double-minded. Not particularly wanting to admit to double-mindedness or to be called hypocrites, we might settle for the label of terrible sinners. After all, it seems reasonable enough. At this point the devil reasons with us further: "Okay, if you admit you are a sinner but not a double-minded sinner or a hypocritical sinner, then you should at least sin openly and honestly."

Such stupidity actually exists. Many so-called Christians have been duped into accepting this nonexistent virtue. Many justify their sins simply because they don't hide them. They have fallen victim to another satanic ploy.

It all comes back to the same point of conflicting confusion: We are sinners, but we are not supposed to sin. Is that really a conflict? Not in the light of Scripture: "My dear children, I write this to you so that you will not sin. But if anybody does sin, we have one who speaks to the Father in our defense—Jesus Christ, the Righteous One. He is the atoning sacrifice for our sins, and not only for ours but also for the sins of the whole world" (1 John 2:1-2).

Why then do some still insist on being robbed of complete forgiveness? Is it because after they have sought and received this forgiveness they sinned again, even before they were off their knees, by "thinking" it all through again?

To Think It Is Not to Do It—It's Only Another Conflict

Another reason some of us are robbed of the fullness of His forgiveness is that we allow ourselves to believe that "To think it is just as bad as to do it." The devil might even suggest that Jesus said this. He never said that! There is a vast difference between thinking *of* a sin and thinking *on* a sin! The former is not sinning; the latter is. When we recall a sin and then embellish it, it becomes sinful.

The thought is nothing more than a temptation. To be tempted is not sin, but to yield to the temptation is a sin. If all of this were not the case, then Christ would *not* have been sinless, for surely He was tempted as we are.

It is truly sad to note how many people go around hating themselves and kicking themselves in the pants every time an evil thought (temptation) pops into their minds. Jesus said, "Anyone who looks at a woman lustfully has already committed adultery with her in his heart" (Matt. 5:28). Notice that he did not say that looking on a woman was adultery or sinful. To think of a sin is only to be tempted. Paul said, "Consider it pure joy . . . whenever you face trials of many kinds, because you know that the testing of your faith develops perseverance [patience]" (James 1:2).

The devil doesn't really make any headway on these points until he can catch us unconsciously or subliminally embellishing a past sin for which we have already been forgiven. Then he'll drive us right up the wall trying to remember to forget. He'll suggest, "Why don't you just admit you enjoy sinning? Eliminate the church and all its silly rules that make your enjoyment and happiness a sin."

Conflicts of Circumstance

Often we credit a series of circumstances (that fall into place in a supernatural way) to God's will, saying, "I wanted to do this or that, and God arranged it so that one thing led to another and everything worked out beautifully, so it must be His will". The devil has the power to do the same thing in your life. Look at what he did to Job.

God leads us through His Word, not necessarily through convenient circumstances although He may arrange things for us *if* what we seek to do is His will. Circumstances (things working out) do not, by themselves, constitute a revelation of God's will. It could just as easily be the devil setting us up for a fall! God's will is revealed in the Bible— nowhere else!

Our Lord's entire mission was directed toward the fact

that you and I are continual, contemptible, vile, disreputable sinners who persistently fail! This doesn't shock Christ, and we should never forget it. The fact that we hang on to guilt feelings after the guilt is gone is stupid and senseless, but it is not shocking to God. The fact that we remember old sins seems quite normal to Him. The fact that the good that we would, we do not do, and the evil that we wouldn't do, we do, is disgustingly carnal; but it doesn't stun God. The fact that we "credit" Him with a devil's set of circumstances is an indication that we really don't understand His will, but this doesn't turn God away from us!

Our comfort is that God understands every detail of each problem. He knows we "all have sinned and fall short" (Rom. 3:23). He realizes tenacity. He knows our frame and how shallow we really are and that "we are all as an unclean thing, and all our righteousnesses are as filthy rags" (Isa. 64:6, KJV).

The point is, He wants *us* to know it too so that we can better understand His words: "For the Son of Man came to seek and to save what was lost" (Luke 19:10). This means you and me! God wants us to understand the one thought behind John 3:17, 1 Timothy 1:15, and Hebrews 7:25: Christ's substitution!

Because "there is none that doeth good, no, not one" (Ps. 53:3, KJV), God gave us grace to live with sin (not in it) through His forgiveness (Gal. 3:13). Sin is a fact of life, the result of which (sins) Christ came to forgive and conquer (Heb. 2:9, 9:28; 1 Pet. 2:24) by substituting Himself instead of giving us what we deserved.

Every time we (in Christ) defeat the devil, we get a little taste of the sweet victory that was His on the cross and will one day be ours in glory through our Lord and Savior, Jesus Christ. God will always supply us the way of escape. "No temptation has seized you except what is common to man. And God is faithful; he will not let you be tempted beyond [or above] what you can bear. But when you are tempted, he will also provide a way out so that you can stand up under it [and be able to bear it]" (1 Cor. 10:13).

With that promise, we can leave Paul's words, "What a wretched man I am! Who will rescue me from this body of death?" (Rom. 7:24), and join him in God's grace, "Therefore, there is now no condemnation for those who are in Christ Jesus" (Rom. 8:1).

What is our responsibility in all this? Is it to cease from ever sinning again? Of course not. Is it to live sinless lives? Yes! Remember, it is more important to live in the joy of God's approval than in the fear of His disapproval. How can this be done? Through forgiveness, but with repentance and confession.

Jesus taught us how He forgives (and how we are supposed to forgive): "If he [anyone] sins against you seven times in a day, and seven times comes back to you and says, 'I repent,' forgive him" (Luke 17:4). Isn't it obvious by now that if we seek forgiveness by repenting, God will forgive? Isn't it also obvious that God will only forgive us if we seek forgiveness by repenting? Because so many neglect forgiveness, our Lord used the threat of hell throughout His ministry (Luke 16:19–31).

This business of forgiveness compounds itself as we grow in sanctification. The closer we walk with Him, the more we realize the depth of our sinfulness and our need for even greater forgiveness.

Before we can hope to witness convincingly, we must have experienced forgiveness ourselves. If you lack such assurance, fall to your knees right now with a Bible and pray the words of Psalm 51. Then turn to and claim the promises of 1 John 1:9. Next read Isaiah 57:18, and then rejoice with the psalmist and with all Christians in these words from God: "The Lord is nigh unto them that are of a broken heart; and saveth such as be of a contrite spirit" (Ps. 34:18, KJV). Rejoice in the words of Jesus Himself: "Neither do I condemn you . . . Go now and leave your life of sin" (John 8:11). Thank Him once and for all for awakening and rescuing you.

We can all live full and free in the joy of our salvation, knowing our personal weaknesses just a little bit better in our world of sin. We can be confident that the "way of escape" spoken of in 1 Corinthians 10:13 is God's inspired Word. Through it we can learn to avoid evil forces by becoming filled with the Holy Spirit's vigor.

8

How to Be Filled with the Holy Spirit

Someone once told me *never* to use terms such as *never*, *always*, *everyone*, and *no one*, but his advice contained a violation of his own standards. So it is with the Christian life. Bible-studying Christians—every one of them—have experienced contradiction, emptiness, depression, and even periods when they turned from God. No Christian is exempt from these phenomena—none, ever. We all need to be filled and refilled with the Holy Spirit.

Since I am a practicing dentist, patients come in to see me every day with decayed teeth. I remove the decay, but that's only the first step. You wouldn't think of leaving a dental office after the "drilling" is completed without the filling, would you—or would you? Certainly not! Because an open tooth without a filling would decay in a very short time.

So it is with the forgiveness (cleansing) from sin. That's only step number one. We must be protected by the filling of the Holy Spirit. God's "dentistry" is painless; we human dentists are still working on that little detail.

You need the Holy Spirit's filling more often than you need your teeth filled; so we don't want to carry this comparison too far. But we *could*: God has X-ray vision that finds the hidden sin and decay in our lives. His "restorations" far exceed "silver or gold." We call His drill the Bible—"quick, and powerful, and sharper than any twoedged sword, piercing even to the . . . joints and marrow" (Heb. 4:12, KJV). And God doesn't use anesthetic; His fillings are painless. Let's make our filling appointment right now!

How to Be Filled with the Holy Spirit

I am writing here in a very personal style since the subject is something each of us must do daily—in some cases even hourly.

The first step in being filled with the Holy Spirit is to reassure yourself that He's in your heart. You may be acknowledging Christ as Savior but not as Lord and Master. We should make certain that we understand all the Scriptures say about the Holy Spirit. These three requirements constitute our initial step.

Second, ask Him to become the Lord of your life by completely resigning yourself to Him. Why not do so now? What has prevented you from doing this long ago? Have you been hanging on to something that you know God wants you to release? Maybe all He wants is your willingness to let it go if He should demand it. He might, but this must be an unconditional surrender on your part; He will not be Lord of your life on a partnership basis. He will only be Lord—Master—if you surrender everything to Him and give Him all the controls. Is there really anything you must retain that He didn't give or create in the first place? You really can't *own* anything for eternity in this life anyway, and nothing is of such value as to prevent His Holy Spirit from filling you to

His fullness because of it. Think it over for a few minutes right now. Truly consider this step before going any further. This is not a loan; it's for keeps. The Holy Spirit (*in you*) is probably bringing to your mind the inevitable matter(s) at this very moment. Allow these thoughts to develop. Let go of whatever He wants you to get rid of, and trust Jesus. He knows all about you, your past, and your future. Put it all in His hands now, once and for all.

Third, clean house. Tell God that He can have whatever you were trying to save in your life. God only fills clean vessels. Confess all known sins to Him by writing them down on a piece of paper. Spend time thinking and writing out every way you have grieved the Holy Spirit or sinned against God both knowingly and unknowingly. Include all those sins that have prevented you from demonstrating the nine manifestations of His Spirit (Gal. 5:22) in your life prior to this day. Include those areas that you have just surrendered. God said, "If a man cleanses himself from the latter [wickedness], he will be an instrument for noble purposes, made holy, useful to the Master and prepared to do any good work" (2 Tim. 2:21). God fills cracked vessels, but they must be clean. Write out your sins before reading on. After you have made a list of every sin you can possibly think of (the first probably being your unwillingness even to put them down on paper), write out the promise of 1 John 1:9 in large letters over the entire list. Now destroy it for no one to ever see because these sins are now gone forever. New Christians have to do the same thing. Peter said, "Repent and be baptized . . . so that your sins may be forgiven. And you will receive the gift of the Holy Spirit" (Acts 2:38). In the case Peter is pointing to here, the baptism and the filling might be thought of as happening simultaneously.

Fourth, give up. Give up trying to make it your way alone,

trying to be good enough. Give up trying not to sin because you know you will again and again, but now you know how to handle these sins. Confess them—just as soon as you commit them—to God "Who forgiveth all thine iniquities; who healeth all thy diseases" (Ps. 103:3, kjv) and who also said, "If we confess our sins, he is faithful and just and will forgive us our sins and purify us from all unrighteousness" (1 John 1:9). We must not become discouraged in the knowledge that we will sin again. God said, "My dear children, I write this to you so that you will not sin. But if anybody does sin [and we know we will], we have one who speaks to the Father in our defense—Jesus Christ, the Righteous One. He is the atoning sacrifice for our sins, and not only for ours but also for the sins of the whole world" (1 John 2:1–2).

Knowing how to handle your sins is one thing; knowing how to avoid them is another. Admit that you're a loser (dead) when it comes to sin but a winner (alive) in Jesus Christ! In other words, let *Him* keep you from sinning instead of trying to do it yourself (1 Cor. 10:13). Don't ask Him just to help you; rather ask Him to become your atoning sacrifice, your substitution, before the Father (not of your personality because He will always honor what He has created you to be, but rather a substitution for the perfection God demands). Submit yourself completely to Him in full surrender, and be filled with His complete victory! "Count yourselves dead to sin but alive to God in Christ Jesus" (Rom. 6:11). His victory is complete and sweet even though giving up may seem bitter at first. Have you ever seen a miserable Christian in the middle of God's victory? "He who did not spare his own Son, but gave him up for us all—how will he not also, along with him, graciously give us all things?" (Rom. 8:32). This includes His fullness. Trust by surrendering to Him. Take self out of it and submit so that you can be pure because HE obeyed. Christ already lived the obedient life (that you can't live) for you, instead of you, in your name, for your benefit, and to your credit. Exchange lives now. Take His. Give up trying to match Him by accepting Him instead (Ps. 27:1). "Thanks be to God for his indescribable [unspeakable] gift! " (2 Cor. 9:15)—His sinless life for yours, His perfection for your imperfection.

Fifth, ask God to fill you now with His Holy Spirit, thus making you fully aware of His baptism in your heart. God will. He commanded you to ask Him for this. He tells you to be filled with the Holy Spirit in Ephesians 5:18. He never asks you to do anything against His will; therefore, He will accomplish it if you will only ask. Jesus said, "If you then, though you are evil, know how to give good gifts to your children, how much more will your Father in heaven give the Holy Spirit to those who ask him!" (Luke 11:13). Ask. Of course, this request must be sincere and must be preceded by a full confession of all sins (the list) so that your vessel is clean. The filling will then be instantaneously accomplished because God said it would be. The next step now becomes joyfully necessary.

Sixth, thank Him. Thank Him in the same breath that you asked Him to fill you. Prove your faith by thanking Him for what He promised He would do and therefore has done. Now open your eyes and believe that God did fill you. Believe it whether you *feel* differently or not. God works with facts, not feelings. He said He would fill you; therefore, He did fill you. If you feel nothing, there may be a perfectly acceptable reason. Perhaps this is the first time you ever totally gave your old life to Jesus Christ. He is now a part of your old life, and as you grow in Him, He will grow in you. As He grows within, your vessel capacity will increase in size (sanctification) so that each filling will be just as full, but the capacity will be greater and, no doubt, more noticeable. This is why feelings are not important at the outset. Just know you are filled; then praise Him and begin walking in the Spirit. "Therefore, there is now no condemnation for those who are in Christ Jesus, . . . who . . . live . . . according to the Spirit" (Rom. 8:1, 4) even though you remain you in the strictest sense.

Walking in the Spirit, Living According to the Spirit, Modifying Yourself

"Live by the Spirit, and you will not gratify [or fulfill] the desires [lusts] of your sinful nature" (Gal. 5:16). Paul also said, "Since we live by the Spirit, let us keep in step [walk] with the Spirit" (Gal. 5:25). To ignore this is to quench and grieve the Holy Spirit.

How can we walk in the Spirit? Before we can understand what this means, we will have to understand that sin (singular) continues, but our sins (plural) are gone. Sin is here, a fact, but our sins are all gone, a greater fact. Walking in the Spirit is walking in a sinless state, not because we do not sin, but because our sins are forgiven! "You are not under law, but under grace" (Rom. 6:14).

"For it is by grace you have been saved, through faith" (Eph. 2:8). But there's a deeper meaning to grace, and walking in the Spirit is a perfect expression of it. Grace means to be accepted in spite of being unacceptable. Grace replaces the penalty of the law which is dead. "So, my brothers, you also died to the law through the body of Christ" (Rom. 7:4). That's grace.

The law is holy (Rom. 7:12–13) and spiritual (Rom.

7:14–18) but produces inner conflicts for those not walking in the Spirit (Rom. 7:19–23). Jesus changed all that (Rom. 7:24–25) and made the law null and void to those walking in the Spirit (Rom. 8:1). "Because through Christ Jesus the law of the Spirit of life set me free from the law of sin and death" (Rom. 8:2). That's grace!

Sin continues even though sins are always forgivable; so being filled with the Holy Spirit cannot be a once in a lifetime experience! For many Christians, being filled may have to be an hourly event.

The frequency of the filling depends on how severely our vessel is cracked. The beautiful thing about the Holy Spirit is that His presence has a mending effect on the crack. Keep the vessel filled, hourly if necessary, until the defect is mended. The whole process of walking in the Spirit will become easier. First, we must crawl, like a car in first gear, knowing only that there is a God—the first Person of the Trinity. Second, we walk and stumble in our own strength, hanging on to everything in sight, knowing about Christ but not knowing the full extent of His power in our lives. Like the second gear of a car, we are going faster but with a noticeable strain. Finally, we shift into third and are able to walk in "high" with the Spirit. The "clutch" is prayer, for only through prayer will the shift take place.

Thus far in our study of the total witness, we've touched on all three Persons of the Trinity. We've considered the act of witnessing as an extension of Christ's personality through our personalities. We've looked at the varied personalities of those He chose to make His disciples and compared their traits with Christ's. Then we considered our Lord as both God-Man and brought into focus the love of God the Father through Jesus Christ in giving us His Son, His gift of faith, and what faith really is. Then we concentrated on the Holy

Spirit as a force for good, then the devil as a force for evil, followed by God's command to each person to be filled with the Holy Spirit. And now, being filled, we can witness fruitfully.

The aim of these first chapters has been to help you better understand Christian beliefs and your own Christian life. With this basis you can be a more effective witness, and you can refer to these chapters for information you might need in witnessing situations.

9

Jesus Christ—The Messiah

Sooner or later you are likely to witness to those who respect the Old Testament as interesting cultural history but do not believe in the New Testament Christ. Some may raise tricky questions about the relationship between the Old and New sections, arguing that they contradict each other by presenting different Gods. Therefore, you should be equipped to equate the Jesus Christ of New Testament times with the promised Messiah of the Old Testament. In so doing you demonstrate the full unity of the Scriptures.

How do you witness to a nonbeliever beginning with the Old Testament? Remember our ninth hitchhiker? "The name of Jesus Christ," he told us, "stuck in my throat like a bone. I couldn't say His name." Yet he understood some of the Old Testament; so we pointed him to Jesus there, using the following format. Becoming acquainted with the major passages should help you capitalize on more opportunities than ever before.

Jesus, as the "Word become flesh," is mirrored throughout Scripture. In Genesis, Abraham (as an earthly father) was asked by God (our heavenly Father) to sacrifice his son Isaac. That duty was similar to God's later action with Jesus!

And God allowed Abraham three days to think it over. Abraham would have given up his son in obedience, but God supplied a substitutionary sacrifice. Isaac was Abraham's only son (Gen. 22:2), and Jesus is God's only Son (John 3:16). The substitution for Isaac was a male lamb called a ram (Gen. 22:13), and Jesus is referred to throughout Scripture as "the lamb of God" (John 1:29). God told Abraham, a Jew, "In thy seed shall all the nations of the earth be blessed; because thou hast obeyed my voice" (Gen. 22:18, KJV). Jesus Christ is Abraham's seed. Some evidence exists that the mountain of Isaac's near sacrifice was the one upon which Jesus was crucified.

In Exodus 12 we read that God offered the Israelites an escape from His judgment. God instructed them to paint their doors with blood from a male lamb without blemish and the angel of death would pass over them. The New Testament portrays Jesus Christ as the Lamb of God without sin (blemish) who shed His blood. When? During the Passover!

We read that God promised David an eternal throne to be established forever (2 Sam. 7:16). Surely this promise did not imply that David himself would be king for eternity; rather the imperishable throne would be perpetuated for all time through David's future seed. One thousand years later, Jesus, the Son of David, was born. Notice the very first words of the New Testament: "A record of the genealogy of Jesus Christ, son of David, son of Abraham" (Matt. 1:1).

We also find Jesus in the psalms. God gave the psalmist an insight into the dying words of Jesus one thousand years in advance: "My God, my God, why hast thou forsaken me?" (Ps. 22:1, KJV). Jesus Christ the Messiah repeated that phrase exactly (Matt. 27:46). The psalmist wrote: "He trusted on the Lord that he would deliver him: let him deliver him" (Ps. 22:8, KJV). One thousand years later, Matthew recorded these words spoken about Jesus Christ at His crucifixion: "He trusted in God; let him deliver him now" (Matt. 27:43, KJV). Again, in Psalms we read: "They pierced my hands and my feet" (Ps. 22:16, KJV). They did that very thing to Jesus Christ on the cross. How could Jesus be anything but the Messiah spoken of in the psalms? "They part my garments . . . and cast lots upon my vesture" (Ps. 22:18), and "They . . . parted his garments, casting lots" (Matt. 27:35, KJV). "They gave me also gall for my meat; and in my thirst they gave me vinegar to drink" (Ps. 69:21, KJV), and centuries later Matthew reported of the crucifixion that "they gave him vinegar to drink mingled with gall" (Matt. 27:34, KJV).

Remember the words of Christ? "The stone which the builders rejected, . . . is become the head of the corner" (Matt. 21:42, KJV). Jesus Christ was rejected, and he repeated the words found in Psalm 118:22. This is the Messiah!

Now let's read Isaiah. Many do not accept the virgin Mary as Isaiah's referent: "A virgin will be with child and will give birth to a son, and will call him Immanuel" (Isa. 7:14). Yet God, through the angel, spoke these very words to Joseph: "The virgin will be with child and will give birth to a son, and they will call him Immanuel—which means 'God with us' " (Matt. 1:23). Isaiah said, " 'Many of them will stumble; and they will fall and be broken, and be snared and be captured.' Bind up the testimony and seal up the law among my disciples" (Isa. 8:15–16). In the New Testament we read: " 'A stone that causes men to stumble and a rock that makes them fall.' They stumble because they disobey the message —which is also what they were destined for" (1 Pet. 2:8). Isaiah spoke about a key of David's house that opens and shuts heaven. Revelation reminds us that this key belongs to Jesus Christ as the head of the church (Isa. 22:22; Rev. 3:7). As a sign to all unbelievers God said that "with . . . strange tongues God will speak to this people" (Isa. 28:11). Today this "other tongue" is referred to as speaking in tongues. Paul confirms this as the sign to the Jews spoken of in Isaiah: "Tongues, then, are a sign, not for believers but for unbelievers" (1 Cor. 14:22). Who are "they"? Every unbeliever!

The Old Testament twice mentions a voice crying in the wilderness (Isa. 40:3; Mal. 3:11). The New Testament introduces us to John the Baptist as "the voice of one crying in the wilderness" (Matt. 3:3, KJV), preparing the way for the Messiah, Jesus Christ, the Son of God.

Every day that goes by is another day lost to the doubter who refuses to recognize his Messiah in the Person of Jesus Christ. He should prayerfully consult Isaiah 53. The problem is this: Non-Christians won't read anything about Jesus Christ unless Christians of today invite them to study both Testaments and bind up the testimony of Isaiah 8:16—even if it's in the back seat of a rented car.

There is more, and for anyone interested in searching the Old Testament further to discover Jesus Christ, be alerted to God's forecast that He would be born in Bethlehem (Mic. 5:2); that He would go to Egypt (Hos. 11:1); that He would live in Galilee (Isa. 9:1, 2); that His coming would be announced by an "Elijah-like" herald (Mal. 3:1, 4:5); that He would teach in parables (Ps. 78:2); that He would be a "smitten Shepherd" (Zech. 13:7) and betrayed (Zech. 11:12–13). The reader might also like to peruse Isaiah 7:13; Joel 2:28, 32; Amos 9:11–12; Daniel 2; Haggai 2:6; Isaiah 40:5–11; and Zechariah 3:8–9, 9:9, 11:12, 12:8, 10, 13:1.

The Old Testament is a factual account of Jesus Christ,

inspired hundreds of years prior to His life on earth by the
only One who could write future events—Almighty God.

God's Spirit now urges us to a broader awareness of
communicating this Jesus. Does it sound like "work"? Does it
appear awesome, religious, serious, even sacred? Does it
sound boring? Witnessing need not be so. Our Lord had fun
doing it, and we should enjoy some of the afterglow (even
the humor) too. Witnessing is not frivolous to be sure, but
it's not putting on a pseudo-pious, dispassionate face either.
Witnessing is nothing more than a bubbling over of what
you really are inside, and that's not *all* sobriety!

10

Smile When You Witness

Although we have no direct record of Jesus laughing, various scriptural accounts imply that our Lord had a real sense of humor. We recognize the awesomeness of His majesty to the point of nearly equating laughter with irreverence. That makes it difficult to enjoy God or, more specifically, our Lord's humor. This is a false notion. God said that there is "a time to laugh" (Eccles. 3:4, KJV), even during a witness. Lightheartedness here and there may put our contact at ease and will attract him to this gentle and beautiful dimension of our Savior's personality.

You will have to use some imagination as you read this chapter; so put away your cares and put on your smile. Be joyful in the Lord as we observe some of the lighter moments Jesus enjoyed in His relationships with people.

Picture Zacchaeus perched up in a tree, ingeniously overcoming his problem of shortness. He wasn't the only one with a good view; Jesus could see him better this way too. He called him down from the tree. Can't you just see this short-legged man scampering out of the branches and undoing all he had just accomplished? Here was a little guy decamping as fast as his tiny, nervous legs would take him, and Jesus yelled up, "Make haste!" When Zacchaeus finally got to the ground, Jesus was probably laughing, for we read that Jesus received him joyfully (Luke 19:6, KJV).

But we must interrupt the humor for a moment and glean our Lord's underlying motive. Divine humor is unique; there is always purpose in it. Jesus didn't call Zacchaeus down out of the tree just to be amusing. Zacchaeus was the chief publican, and that was pretty serious. Twice in succession Christ classified publicans with harlots (Matt. 21:31–32).

That day Jesus was in Jericho, a city filled with "good" priests; yet He chose to spend the night with a "sinner," a nonbelieving tax collector. He not only called him out of the tree but publicly announced that He would stay overnight with him. The humor was gone for those who saw it. Jesus had passed up church leaders for a sinner (Luke 19:7), illustrating the truth that He had come to save sinners.

On another occasion, perhaps preoccupied with what had happened earlier that day, Jesus was witnessing to His disciples and said, "Be careful, . . . Be on your guard against the yeast of the Pharisees and Sadducees" (Matt. 16:6). Out of a clear blue sky, He said that and no more.

Just before this, His disciples had realized among themselves that they had failed to bring bread along. They were clear over on the "other side" when they received that awful feeling which comes upon remembering that something has been forgotten. Therefore, Jesus' words "Be on your guard against the yeast of the Pharisees and Sadducees" hit the wrong chord.

Naturally, they began to discuss and reason among themselves: "It is because we didn't bring any bread" (Matt. 16:7). No doubt they felt exposed and wondered how He knew. At this point Jesus perceived what a mess they had made of His profoundly intended statement and, no doubt with a smile on His face, set them straight (Matt. 16:8–12).

Once in a while, Jesus used absurdity while witnessing, mixing it with a little humor. Consider the mental pictures He painted for us: a house built on shifting sand, falling to pieces; the face of a child who asked for bread and received a stone instead; the two blind men leading each other along the street until they both ended up in the gutter, totally disoriented.

In another case, Jesus chided, Why do you go around worrying about trouble? Don't you have enough already? He said it in these words: "Do not worry about tomorrow, for tomorrow will worry about itself. Each day has enough trouble of its own" (Matt. 6:34).

One time He told us to quit looking for the slivers in someone else's eye when we have a "two by four" in our own eye (see Luke 6:41). He had to be kidding here; yet the lesson behind his statement is all too clear.

Have you ever been told "Do what I say, not what I do" or "They say one thing and do another"? Jesus uttered both of these popular sayings and meant them to be humorously instructive in His witness (Matt. 23:3).

After rebuking the scribes and Pharisees, He said, "You strain out a gnat but swallow a camel" (Matt. 23:24). Can you recall the fuss you made the last time some little bug flew into your open throat? A little gnat can elicit an enormous gag reflex. If he isn't choking to death, it is rather funny to note the expression on a person's face as he grasps his throat and gulps, "I just swallowed a bug!" All the while his eyes are bugging out of his head. During His witness, Jesus said, "You strain out a gnat but swallow a camel."

Remember impetuous Peter? He saw Jesus walking on the water and wanted to try it too. After all, it looked like fun.

Peter made an unsophisticated request: "Lord, if it's you, . . . tell me to come to you on the water" (Matt. 14:28). Knowing that Peter would begin to wonder soon enough how he was accomplishing this feat, Jesus complied and said, "Come." No doubt Jesus knew Peter would "blow it."

We can only guess at how many steps Peter took before he looked around, taking his eyes off Jesus and seeing the fantastic size of the waves, probably with white spray blowing off their tops. Frightened, Peter began to doubt the buoyancy of the whole affair and started to sink; so he cried to Jesus for help.

As always, Jesus was right there. He knew Peter better than Peter understood himself. The Bible tells us that Jesus caught Peter immediately, without letting him sink down to his neck first. Fear had to be written all over his face as the Bible notes (Matt. 14:30). We should observe something else here. Peter didn't realize he was in trouble and then carefully calculate whether he should ask Christ for help. There wasn't time. Nor did Peter do what too many of us do—begin his prayer with three tons of verbalism. There wasn't time. He simply screamed, "Lord, save me!" Jesus did "immediately" (Matt. 14:31).

But Jesus didn't address Himself to the look of fear on Peter's face; He looked beyond the obvious as He always does and said, "You of little faith, why did you doubt?" The Bible doesn't tell us what, if anything, Peter had to say, but we can imagine Jesus taking him under one armpit and raising one shoulder above the other to emphasize Peter's helplessness, as we do with our children when they fall face first in the mud. The Bible says, "Immediately Jesus reached out his hand and caught him." It was rather embarrassing to say the least, but that's what often happens to impulsive people.

Peter still had "egg on his face"; he didn't get wet enough to wash it off!

Many times Christ's humor in witnessing drew on the apparent. We were all created with two eyes, two ears, one nose, and one mouth. We all stand before our Creator with two ears sticking out from our heads; yet Christ would often end His dialogue (perhaps even with a smile) saying, "He that hath ears, let him hear." The humor involved can't obscure Christ's obvious warning that His words demand attention.

At times we must inadvertently humor God as we decide all by ourselves that we are going to do this or that for Him, forgetting that we cannot do anything of ourselves. At other times we undoubtedly concern Him when we decide all by ourselves that *we* will do some witnessing for God instead of relying on His Spirit to use us. This must appear to Him to be very much like a little boy stumbling into the living room, carrying several large pieces of wood, a saw, hammer, and some nails. He announces to his parents that all by himself he is going to build a big house for mom and dad. Obviously, he believes that he can build it right in their living room. This is amusing, but what a pity to misunderstand so completely.

Finally, Christ specifically asked us not to recite our prayers. He gave us the Lord's Prayer as a guide or an outline. He told us, "After this manner therefore pray ye" (Matt. 6:9–13, KJV). So what do we do? We memorize the outline and recite it back to Him repetitiously.

We should carefully avoid such silliness in witnessing too. When you come to the prayer of commitment and the new convert feels he cannot pray spontaneously aloud in front of you, have him repeat out loud a prayer of commitment that you organize on the spot. Prefabricated prayers lack the

Spirit's input. Just as each individual is different, each individual prayer of commitment should be different.

Smile and be at peace with yourself while witnessing. Be alert to the distinctive needs of those to whom you speak while concentrating on a specific message—God's plan of salvation.

11

Some Specifics on Witnessing

This chapter deals with an outline for presenting Christ. Assuming we know just about what we want to say, in what order are we going to say it? How should we say it? How did we get ourselves into this in the first place?

Discipleship

How did we ever get involved in witnessing? Discipleship! We have a mandate to witness but also a mandate to "sin not." As we have seen, a command by itself does not insure obedience. Acceptance of any requirement is only validated in performance. Faith without works is dead, and this "work" is not easy.

A price must be paid when witnessing *for* Jesus, and we may be called upon to pay it. Jesus would ask each person who is ready to begin working for Him, "Have you counted the cost? Are you sure you want to? It may mean exchanging everything you now have for me."

As followers of Jesus, we should be ready to leave everything of importance. Jesus said, "If anyone comes to me and does not hate his father and mother, his wife and children, his brothers and sisters—yes, even his own life—he cannot be my disciple. And anyone who does not carry his cross and follow me cannot be my disciple" (Luke 14:26–27). These are strong words. Certainly Christ is not telling us to hate our families. But if allegiance to family ever prevents a full commitment, we may be called upon to reject one and love the other. Jesus said that we cannot serve two masters. This is really no surprise, is it?

Jesus loves us enough to warn us forcefully about our involvement in obeying him. He told us about tower-builders who didn't sit down to count the cost before beginning. Before anyone declares his availability for witnessing, he would be wise to sit down first and count the entire cost. It could be heavy. Jesus also talked about salt that loses its saltiness (Luke 14:34–35). As great as our eagerness may be, Jesus wants us to realize what may happen to our zeal when the chips are down. Salt without saltiness isn't even fit for the manure pile, Jesus said!

The warning comes to us in love. God does not want us to jump in with wild enthusiasm and try to conquer the whole world for Him before preparing ourselves; even then, He surely doesn't need *us* to "make Him famous". He could make stones cry out if He chose.

How Should We Say It?

We have a lot to tell the world about Jesus. How are we going to say it? A "worldly" person may not realize his or her need for a Savior; so maybe we should first ask ourselves what constitutes a "witness." Is it pasting a bumper sticker on the car? Going to church on Sunday? Telling someone else to worship regularly? Producing a Christian movie? Handing out "Don't Swear" cards, or *telling* someone not to swear and then running away as fast as I did when I was a boy?

Each of the above is a witness, everything we do (good or bad) is a witness (Matt. 12:30). Some ways of saying it, however, are more productive than others. Our duty is to find and use these methods because none of the techniques mentioned above really deals with the nitty-gritty of introducing Jesus Christ to someone as the solution to *his* problem. Bumper stickers that read "Jesus is the solution" make me cringe at the world's probable conjecture: What's the problem? The solution to what? A lost soul faced with serious problems might see this slogan and assume Jesus could do him some good at the moment. Suppose that this person decides to give Him a try, only to learn later—much to his chagrin—that Jesus is no solution apart from personal commitment. How is he supposed to know this ahead of time unless we tell him? A major defect in "bumper-sticker evangelism" is that it doesn't give *us* a chance to say anything.

Most of us are lazy enough to welcome three or four (or even ten) easy steps to help us know *how to say it*, but this is a symptom of our apprehension. God gave us His witness in sixty-six books, not in a reduced number of universal steps. In spite of this, we come up with a few shortcuts and a few canned procedures, but these methods don't really let us say it either. They tend to deny the fact that God entrusted us with His holy Word as our witnessing tool.

The best way to "say it" is to be steeped in His Word so deeply that when someone asks us about the "hope within us" the witness just bubbles out. Being available to witness and knowing how to "say it" mean we have studied God's Word and recorded it in our hearts through memorization.

Witnessing is basically an overflow from diligent Bible study, a brimming over of deep, heartfelt convictions.

If God's total witness is already found in the Bible, one might question whether any of us need to witness verbally. Indeed, some distribute the Scriptures and say no more. As we've already seen, some also insist that we are not required ever to witness verbally. Static methods of presenting Jesus, however, are far less than ideal. God made that lesson vivid and unmistakable when He sent Philip to *explain* the Scriptures. This is what witnessing is all about—having the Scriptures come alive through us by making them understandable in their total context.

Another reason God entrusted us with speaking His message is that people respond to people better than they relate to the printed page. When the U.S. prisoners of war were released from North Vietnam, American armed forces sent in personal escorts for each prisoner with the backgrounds, personalities, and the interests of each matched as closely as possible. I believe that God has been doing that same thing ever since Pentecost—matching personalities in witnessing situations. The witnessee, (the person who is witnessed to) can't often explain what it was about the witnesser that caused them to interact well, but we know that it was the Holy Spirit's power. Maybe your next contact will like the way you talk or dress or the way you part your hair, but, through it all, Jesus Christ will come through. This is why canned or static methods are not ideal beyond the learning stage.

God may have entrusted us with His Good News to force us into Scripture study before passing it on. Searching Scripture is as essential to the witnesser in preparation as it is to the witnessee in hearing the actual presentation. As convenient as it may be to begin with written aids, it soon becomes necessary to graduate into the fuller power of the Holy Spirit. The confidence we require to witness is the assurance that the Holy Spirit will accomplish His work in the hearts and lives of His people. Confidence in ourselves is not necessary, for there are no failures in witnessing. The man who thinks he's available, without studying Scripture, will not be called upon. In fact, he is the devil's delight because as soon as we go it alone we rely on ourselves and on our feelings, and feelings will betray us every time. Such a process of self-execution suppresses and grieves the Spirit.

In What Order Are We Going to Say It?

We should begin the witness by stating the problem or the bad news so that Jesus, the Good News, can be seen as the solution. In order to witness effectively, we must identify the problem (sin) before the solution (Christ). Many people are fairly content, unaware that they are lost or even have a problem; so presenting them with solutions to nonexistent problems makes us seem rather presumptuous, if not down-right silly.

Sin is not a popular subject, especially when presented as an odious problem. But what problem is popular? We have two kinds of sin: ours (easy to identify) and Adam's (more difficult to make relevant). Let's begin with Adam's original sin.

Original Sin—The Bad News

Original sin is not easily discussed because it all happened thousands of years ago. Many people fail to notice any relationship that original sin may have with them in the twentieth century; so we must describe what happened and how it affects them today. We must explain it in simple, clear, everyday street language, avoiding all confusing theological terminology understood only by mature Christians. Of course, whatever we say must be proved from the Scriptures as well. Original sin aids our witness because it automatically preempts the question, Why would a loving God send anyone to hell? It establishes God's righteousness and the fact that we all justly deserve hell.

Man was created so perfect (sinless) that God said, "Behold, it was very good" (Gen. 1:31, kjv), but man decided to disobey God, and this was sin (Gen. 3:6). God, being just, had no alternative but to punish man (Gen. 3:22–24), and that punishment affects us today. The skeptic will surely ask how. Maybe it is best to answer him in terms he can identify with. Today we know sorrow, pain, death, thorns and thistles, hard labor, selfishness, murder, jealousy, strife, hatred, and, worst of all, separation from God. From a perfect sinless state of harmonious fellowship with God, Adam (because he listened to the devil instead of God) chose (for himself and us) an end to his (and our) perfect relationship with God. Today we carry the effects of Adam's original sin in our sinning as well as Adam's original sin. God tells us that "the result of one trespass [Adam's] was condemnation for all men" (Rom. 5:18). The Bible says, about all of us today, that Adam's sin condemned all men.

> "There is no one righteous, not even one;
>   there is no one who understands,
>   no one who searches for God.
> All have turned away
>   and together become worthless.
> There is no one who does good,
>   not even one."
>
> Rom. 3:10–12

"For all have sinned and fall short of the glory of God" (Rom. 3:23).

Because of original sin and because of our own daily sins, we should allow the witnessee to feel that in his present state of sin he is quite normal. We have *all* sinned, but most worldly people don't really care about original sin or personal sins or even God until they see Jesus and what He did while they were yet sinners. Because we are sinful, it is hopeless to assume that we can have any life whatever with God apart from Jesus Christ. "For the wages of sin is death [damnation and hell], but the gift of God is eternal life through Christ Jesus our Lord" (Rom. 6:23).

At this point your contact may not agree that he is a sinner, or he may question the existence of hell. These tangents (or ploys) of the devil divert the clear presentation of the Person of Jesus Christ. We will talk about *how* to handle them in chapter 13. As one acquires experience in witnessing, it becomes evident that after someone accepts Christ the tangent questions become mute.

The Good News: We Do Not Have to Earn Eternal Life. It Is a Gift.

We can forget about trying to achieve heaven by being good. Jesus did it for us: "Just as through the disobedience of the one man [Adam] the many were made sinners, so also through the obedience of the one man [Jesus Christ] the many will become righteous" (Rom. 5:19). Of His own free choice, Jesus Christ took upon Himself the condemnation, penalty, curse, wrath, and just judgment of God the Father. It was an act of God's grace (Rom. 5:15–21) when Jesus, in obedience, died our death and descended into our hell to pay for our sins. He did this in our place as a gift to us. It is an achievement offered freely and received through faith. "For it is by grace you have been saved, through faith—and this is not from yourselves, it is the gift of God—not by works, so that no one can boast" (Eph. 2:8–9). "For the wages of sin is death, but the gift of God is eternal life through Christ Jesus our Lord" (Rom. 6:23).

You probably understand how Jesus Christ secured eternal life for us, but the person to whom you are witnessing might well ask, "How does Jesus make any difference?" It is essential to know the mind of the witnessee. If the question is, Who is Jesus? some answers are found in chapter 9 of this book.

If, on the other hand, the question refers to "How did He do it?" we should turn to Romans 5:19 where we read that through one man many became righteous and then go right on to 2 Corinthians 5:21: "God made him [Jesus Christ] who had no sin to be sin for us, so that in him we might become the righteousness of God." Jesus Christ exchanged places with us, assuming our sin so that we could become the righteousness of God. The person to whom you are witnessing may have difficulty understanding these texts. You may need to take ten or fifteen minutes to review these two verses word by word, expounding on each word's meaning as best you can by comparing related passages. The ability to expound on Scripture in its total context requires much study. You can begin by taking a concordance and checking the two key words *sin* and *righteousness*. Mark those verses in your Bible (and memory!) which seem especially helpful.

There is a perfect balance between Christ's merits and God's free grace. Jesus said, "Come to me, all you who are weary and burdened, and I will give you rest" (Matt. 11:28). He also promised that "whoever comes to me I will never drive away" (John 6:37). This is God's grace in Christ. "For it is by grace . . . [we] have been saved, through faith" (Eph. 2:8). Therefore, in our presentation we should emphasize the grace of God, His undeserved favor for all who believe.

Up to this point, we have covered the subject of man (who cannot save himself), man's original sin, and his personal sins. We have also explained God's solution to man's problem of sin, the cross of Christ; but so far we haven't really concentrated on the *Person* of Jesus.

Jesus Christ

Jesus Christ was a man, but He is also God. To drive the point home, let's quote John 1:1 somewhat differently: In the beginning was Jesus, and Jesus was with God and Jesus was God.

I am going to assume that everything you've read so far (and the subsequent chapters) will enable you to witness faithfully to His Person at this step in the outline. Later we'll take another look at Jesus in the context of the fruit of the Spirit and how we compare. After that, His environment two thousand years ago will be described. Of course, you will want to add all you know about the Savior from your own study of Scripture.

Faith

Faith is the next subject in the outline. We've already covered this complex subject in chapter five. For our purposes here, I'll merely ask you to flag it as the next topic in your presentation.

The Invitation

No doubt about it! We've arrived at the hardest step. We have told the person about God's grace (that salvation is not earned); about man's original sin, plus our own sins; about God who is merciful but also just; about the human and divine Jesus Christ who paid for our sins (Isa. 53); about faith being intellectually historic or saving in nature. Maybe we exaggerate the difficulty because we fear a rejection. I used to talk and talk so that the witnessee *couldn't* get a no in edgewise. (That was after I quit running!) Now it's time to pop the question, to ask for a commitment.

The easiest way to begin is to summarize quickly what you have said thus far and then add something like this: "Did you know God is right here, now? He's waiting for you to confess Him before men. Would you like to accept Jesus Christ as *your* Savior right now?" Or, "Do you agree that sinners like us need a Savior? Do you agree Jesus Christ *is* that Savior? Do you wish to have Him come into your heart right here and now?" Or, "You have told me your life was one of separation from God. Would you like to know Him better now as your Savior and Lord? Will you give Him your life, right now, today?" Or, "You've heard God's wonderful plan of salvation. Are you ready at this moment to take Jesus Christ as your own Savior?" Or, "You have agreed that we are sinners. Jesus Christ came to pay for sin, yours and mine. Once He's done that and we have accepted Him, then God looks at us through the sinless Jesus and declares us sinless. God will either see us for what we are—sinners to be punished—or sinless in the Christ who already paid for our sins. Are you willing to accept Jesus Christ's sacrifice for you right now?" Or, "God must punish sin. He will either punish you and me as sinners, or he will punish Jesus Christ who took away our sins on the cross. My sins are gone in Christ. Would you also like to be found 'not guilty' in Christ?"

There are all kinds of ways to close the invitation. The most important aspect is to make your statement positive and word it to allow for a simple yes or no answer. Center your question on the acceptance of *Jesus Christ*.

The person you are witnessing to won't laugh at you. The transition between the presentation and the invitation is best made by first reviewing the plan of salvation just given, followed by a definite invitation to receive Jesus Christ here and now, on the spot, with a prayer of commitment.

Church Referrals

Please don't fall into the ploy of presenting the church, your pastor, church membership, or church attendance as *prerequisites* to receiving Christ. Only Jesus saves. To talk someone into church or toward your pastor, before the commitment, only sidesteps the focus on Jesus and comes off as an advocation of piety. It is only too likely that the witnessee may have been turned off by the clergy or the church long ago. Avoid making anyone search for salvation in a church. The church does not save although certainly it *IS* important for proper Christian growth and follow-up.

The general concept of church is vague even among Christians; so we should try to spend some additional time after the commitment defining what the church is (and what it is supposed to be). We speak of two churches: the invisible and the visible. The invisible church is that holy body of true believers from the beginning of time till now, in addition to all who will ever believe prior to Christ's Second Coming. The visible church is the one around the corner, that body of believers presently on earth mixed in with many "dead branches" and phony Christians who give credence to the accusations that the church (meaning visible) is full of pious hypocrites. It is, but, praise God, He loved us while we were still hypocrites.

Too often resistance to the church becomes couched in the excuse that the whole scene isn't necessary for one to honor or worship God. Simply agree for the time being, and move back to the commitment. This might best be accomplished by stating the fact that the church is the bride of Christ and to accept Him without His bride is rather strange. Let the person to whom you are witnessing know that you understand *why* he feels the way he does about the church. Nevertheless, the role of the church in one's spiritual growth remains vital. The future growth of each person to whom you witness depends heavily on his church affiliation. To what kind of a church will you refer him?

Some churches are absolutely dead and cold in their relationship to Jesus Christ. Some are alive and vibrant. A few are so busy bickering and fighting that nothing is accomplished for the kingdom. Others only vaguely mention God as they preach good morals and social niceties. You can usually recognize the "on fire" churches from the "cold" churches by watching how they fish for men's souls. Picture three boats in the water; each represents one of the three kinds of visible churches. In the first boat are the "non-boat-rockers"; in the second boat is a credibly alive group, exerting and exhorting; in the third boat are those whose efforts are dissipated by internal haggling.

Now picture fishermen in each boat. In the first boat sit the "non-boat-rockers," hardly breathing. No one is moving; everything is status quo. Barnacles have grown on the sides of the boat and on their line. Their hooks are empty, but the boat is very peaceful; and that is the way they like it, cool but peaceful.

In the second boat, the "alive" fishermen are active. A lot of work is going on, and they are moving about, comparing notes and results. The boat is rocking a bit because of their activity while landing fish. They are constantly rebaiting their hooks to catch more fish. Some search for fish with shallow methods while others use deeper methods, but all seek to fish!

In the third boat, the hagglers are all standing up, knocking one another over the head with the oars, accusing one another of using the wrong bait. Their boat rocks so badly that it nearly capsizes. The point of contention seems far more important than any fish that might be hooked, and those who are not yet hooked are frightened off by those who are dead on the vine (or line).

The point of all this is to emphasize the importance of the role of the church in the spiritual growth of new and old converts. Without a Christ-centered, Christ-honoring, and Christ-active church, one might well die in the bud of faith. Steer the new convert carefully when recommending a church.

Organization

In an effort to organize your presentation, I have listed a series of texts that might be useful. It is doubtful that you would ever use all of these texts in any given witness because we want to start where the witnessee is spiritually and then move on from there. Also, once the witnessee has accepted a point, there is little need to dwell on the rest of the texts under that point until after he has accepted Christ and we begin our follow-up. In the initial contact move as quickly as possible (without unnecessary rushing, of course) through all the stages in the outline.

It would be a good idea to buy several small, pocket-sized editions of the New Testament. Most will include the psalms as well. Underline the texts listed below, using a color code for each category. After using a copy with a witnessee, give it to him. Tell him you'll be back to study more of God's Word with him in a few days.

Sin

Romans 3:23
Romans 6:23
Romans 3:10
Romans 5:8, 12
Romans 2:11–12
1 John 2:1–2
Acts 2:38
1 John 1:10

Grace

Romans 3:23–25
Ephesians 2:8–9
Romans 6:23
2 Corinthians 5:21
John 6:37
Romans 5:15–21

Jesus Christ

John 1:1
Romans 5:9
1 Peter 1:18
John 1:3
John 1:14
John 17:5

Mark 16:19
Romans 10:4
Matthew 5:17, 20:28

Faith

Romans 10:17
Hebrews 11:1
James 2:17
1 John 5:4
Mark 11:22–26
Romans 5:1
Psalm 27:3, 118:8
Proverbs 3:5

**Abundant Life
in Jesus Christ**

John 10:10
John 8:31–32
Mark 8:36
1 John 5:11
John 20:31
John 3:36
John 3:17
Romans 5:8

1 John 1:5–7
Acts 4:12
1 John 5:13
Acts 1:8

Growth

John 15:7
John 14:27
Romans 8:1
Romans 8:15–16
Colossians 2:14–18

1 Peter 5:6–7
Matthew 22:37–39

Personal Application

John 11:25–26
Luke 9:24–25
Ephesians 2:8–9
1 John 1:9
John 3:16–17
James 2:10
1 John 5:11–13

I think our traveling stranger in the first chapter had a good idea when he encouraged the other person to hold his Bible and to look up each text. We shouldn't laugh if he asks us if Ephesians is before or after Ecclesiastes. We shouldn't even smile. God wouldn't. If there are any questions like this, we can briefly attend to them, remembering not to run off on a tangent. A given witness could take ten to thirty minutes. I remember witnessing in a restaurant once for six continuous hours—with no commitment even then. I've also seen the Holy Spirit bring another to Christ in ten minutes. It depends upon where the witnessee stands in relation to Christ.

Perhaps one of the greatest aids in organizing our witness is as old as Scripture itself. The biggest favor we can ever do ourselves is to commit key texts to memory. It's really too bad that so many agree with that statement but do nothing about it. The rewards are numerous, and the witness improves remarkably. Without key texts in our memory, we tend to fumble around or, even worse, misquote Scripture.

Keeping Score

During war times, pilots painted small enemy flags on the fuselage of their airplanes usually right below the cockpit window. Each flag represented a victory. The whole crew would point with pride at the number of flags it had painted. In the old West, men notched their guns for the same reason: keeping score or taking credit for an achievement.

Woe to the Christian worker who takes credit for souls he's led to Jesus. We are cracked vessels that God uses. Anyone who receives Jesus Christ after something we did or said accepts Him in spite of us. Often the persons to whom we witness will be acutely aware of this. If the person witnessed to feels that the witnesser might consciously or subconsciously want to take credit for it, he may purposefully hold back until he is sure that Jesus Christ will receive the glory. Help him decide for Christ by taking self out of it from the very outset.

Once a person has accepted Jesus, he begins a long road called growth, and you are starting a journey called follow-up—a complete subject in itself and one we will attend to later.

12

Eleven Rules to Follow While Witnessing

1. Begin a witness by asking God to bless the effort and give you the words, the wisdom, and the power of His Holy Spirit. A prayer like this can take any form. It can be short; some are even humorous. I remember the humor in our stranger's prayer before he witnessed to another hitchhiker. I hadn't even seen the shadowlike figure on the highway when my companion blurted out all in one breath: "Hey . . . stop the car, here's another one. Okay, God, here's another one waiting to hear about Your Son Jesus. Tell him all about Jesus through us, okay? Thanks God! Hey, back up a little bit, don't make him run. We want him fresh!" Good thing he said "Thanks God!" or I would have wondered why he wanted God to back up. I never did back up. I couldn't find reverse in that sporty four-on-the-floor!

Prayer before witnessing is essential. We may not leave Him out of the effort when He is the Author and Finisher of our faith as well as the faith of those to whom we witness.

2. Avoid arguing. Arguing only allows the devil to sidetrack the presentation of Jesus Christ by diverting us onto

some insignificant issue. How do you know if the point is worthless or not? It is always trifling if it precedes an acceptance of Jesus Christ. We will consider how to answer all these tangents in the next chapter. Suffice it to say here that many lose the thrust of their message because they were sidetracked about some worthless point and never returned to the subject of Jesus Christ. Instead, they argued.

Usually, one of the last arguments you will hear against accepting Jesus Christ will not be aimed at Christ Himself; it will be an argument about something or someone closely associated with Jesus.

An example would be an argument about how someone (usually someone other than the person complaining) was mistreated by the church at one time or another, or arguing about how the church is filled with hypocrites. The best way to avoid such an argument is to answer the charge from Scripture and then immediately return to the subject of Jesus Christ. A Scripture text that will cover most arguments of this type is found in 2 Peter 3:9: "The Lord is not slow in keeping his promise, as some understand slowness. He is patient with you, not wanting any to perish, but everyone to come to repentance." Another good text to memorize is found in 1 John 1:8–10: "If we claim to be without sin, we deceive ourselves and the truth is not in us. If we confess our sins, he is faithful and just and will forgive us our sins and purify us from all unrighteousness. If we claim we have not sinned, we make him out to be a liar, and his word has no place in our lives."

Yet, there will be times, even when we try not to argue, that we will be forced to deal with one who loves to argue with us. The Bible tells us that " 'in the last times there will be scoffers who will follow their own ungodly desires.' These are the men who divide you, who follow mere natural instincts and do not have the Spirit." Then the Bible goes on to tell us how to handle the arguing person: "Be merciful to those who doubt; snatch others from the fire and save them; to others show mercy, mixed with fear—hating even the clothing stained by corrupted flesh" (Jude 17–23).

There is an enormous difference between arguing and teaching. Paul said, "The Lord's servant must not quarrel; instead, he must be kind to everyone, able to teach, not resentful. Those who oppose him he must gently instruct, in the hope that God will give them a change of heart leading them to a knowledge of the truth" (2 Tim. 2:24–25). This instruction (rule) commands us to witness to someone for years and years if necessary.

3. Stay on the subject of Christ. As bad as it is for the witnessee to sidetrack the witnesser with questions and tangents, it is even worse for the witnesser to sidetrack himself. We do this by taking God's Word and adding to it all kinds of personal testimonies. We should avoid talking about ourselves in the initial stages of evangelism. Testimonies are accounts of what the Lord has done for *us*; witnessing is an account of what the Lord can do for the *witnessee*. The unbeliever may have enough difficulty understanding about Jesus without the added work of trying to comprehend us. Personal statements should only be shared with other Christians. Once the unbeliever accepts Christ, shower him with testimonies; he will then be built up in the faith. Until then, don't confuse him with what God has done for you when your purpose is to emphasize what God will do for him.

Another aspect of this rule of staying on the subject of Christ is to avoid confusing theological jargon. Jargon is incomprehensible to newcomers and has little meaning for most Christians; therefore, strive to spare the witnessee the pain. We must be mindful of words like *grace*, for example. He might ask, "Grace who?"

4. Avoid exalting yourself above the person to whom you are witnessing. Paul said, "Though I am free and belong to no man, I make myself a slave to everyone, to win as many as possible" (1 Cor. 9:19). To those outside the law, Paul was without law; to those who were weak, he became weak; to the Jew, he became a Jew. In other words, Paul was saying, "I make myself equal with those to whom I witness for the sake of the gospel, that the gospel can be seen instead of me."

This is such a simple rule; yet it's so easy to break. The devil finds it a convenient tool to use against the kingdom unless we remember to witness in humility. No matter what our station in life, we are called upon to witness Jesus, not our sanctified selves.

5. Become thoroughly familiar with Scripture so that you can point (with accuracy) to every text used in presenting Jesus. Allow the witnessee to read it for himself. Have the verses marked in your Bible and then leave that Bible for the person to whom you are witnessing. Use some of your tithing money to buy several Bibles each month. Without a working knowledge of Scripture, we can slip into a famous quote and "claim" a biblical origin. It may not be. We must memorize the tool we are using lest we peddle half-truths, morals, or social niceties in error.

6. Avoid taking on the role of the condemner; yet present a full account of the gospel. God is love, but God is also just. There is no Good News without knowledge of the bad news. Balance is the key. Too many well-meaning Christians be-

come preoccupied with negatives in an effort to counter the
avalanche of the positive. Those who insist on driving condemnation home assert, "If a sinner doesn't first realize that
he is a sinner, how can he ever be saved?" They are right,
but the trouble is that they often never leave the first point.
Equilibrium is essential.

Condemnation is God's business, not ours. Our business is
to present the victim of God's condemnation, Jesus Christ.
Jesus did not come into the world just to castigate us. "For
God did not send his Son into the world to condemn the
world, but to save the world through him" (John 3:17).
Jesus is our Savior, not our condemner; yet the full gospel
must be brought to every person in balance and complete-
ness. Jesus Christ is the complete gospel, and the Holy Spirit's ministry is to convict the world of sin and judgment
(John 16:8).

7. The seventh rule may not sound too nice, but it is essential. Avoid allowing someone the "out" of thinking it over.
Giving someone time to ponder things is bad kingdom business. In our business world, giving someone time to consider
the options is responsible, but it is "bad news" while witnessing. Jesus said, "When anyone hears the message about the
kingdom and does not understand it, the evil one comes and
snatches away what was sown in his heart" (Matt. 13:19).
This is God's warning not to let someone think it over for a
while. Now is the acceptable time; today is the day of salvation. If the witnessee is having a problem understanding the
plan of salvation and cannot seem to make up his mind, we
should stay with him and settle the matter even if it delays
our schedule—lest the wicked one would undo everything
and "catch away that which was sown in his heart." "Your

enemy the devil prowls around like a roaring lion looking for someone to devour" (1 Pet. 5:8). By allowing someone time to deliberate unnecessarily, we invite a problem.

8. The eighth rule ties in with the sixth. We must avoid dwelling on the person's past, again bearing in mind that our mission is to present Jesus Christ. It's dangerous to become involved in listening to all the sordid details of another's sin-life! If a person is using his sinful past as a stalling tangent, move him off that subject. (We will see how in a later chapter.) If he is honestly hung-up on his past, he would *welcome* Jesus. With Jesus, the past disappears; so there is no need to dwell on it. In Jesus, he will be a new creature, a new creation; old things will be gone (See 2 Cor. 5:17).

9. After the conversion and during the growing period, avoid presenting standards that you yourself are not living up to, lest you appear a hypocrite. "You, then, who teach [witness to] others, do you not teach yourself? You who preach against stealing, do you steal?" (Rom. 2:21). The responsibility here is grave. Jesus said, "Things that cause people to sin are bound to come, but woe to that person through whom they come. It would be better for him to be thrown into the sea with a millstone tied around his neck than for him to cause one of these little ones to sin" (Luke 17:1–2).

10. Avoid writing someone off as an impossible sinner. Saul said he was the chief of sinners; yet Christ saved him. Saul, as a believer called by his new name Paul, wrote: "Here is a trustworthy saying that deserves full acceptance: Christ Jesus came into the world to save sinners—of whom I

am the worst" (1 Tim. 1:15). I know of a hitchhiker who is thanking God that a stranger didn't dismiss him as too difficult.

11. The last rule of witnessing is to follow up whenever possible. In the case of the hitchhikers, many Bibles were given away during those twenty-four hours. That's about all one could do in that situation. More often than not, we fail to follow up for selfish reasons. We say we're too busy with our children or family or some other good kingdom cause when the truth is we are too busy with ourselves. Following-up is not as painful or involved as it might first appear. The work is that of the Holy Spirit and the textbook is the Bible. All one would really have to do is to take his own personal study time in the Scriptures and include the new convert, unless, of course, one isn't in the Scriptures as he should be.

After we look at some of the common tangents people throw at us during a witness, we will devote more attention to follow-up. But first the tangents people typically employ.

13

Satanic Tangents
in Witnessing

Often, people to whom we witness attempt to sidetrack us onto tangents that have nothing to do with the Person of Jesus Christ. Some of these sidetracks seem related enough to the subject of witnessing that we inadvertently find ourselves off the subject, injecting our own answers over and above (even instead of) Christ's. By allowing the person being witnessed to to divert us, we invite confusion. What would Jesus want us to say to the tangent-seeker? How would He deal with this potential hazard? What does the Bible say about these sidestepping efforts?

The tangent-seeker may be stalling consciously or unconsciously to avoid truth. Don't let him pursue this without reintroducing Jesus Christ as a direct answer to his tangent attempt.

Some will not listen to anything we have to say about Jesus; they enjoy an argument about Him. These tangent-seekers seem unready to accept Jesus Christ; yet they may have a hang-up with which we can deal. We will isolate these now, hoping that the next person who comes along will receive a little better reception because we loved, cared, and pointed him to the gospel without confusing him.

In each category, I will list a few texts even though (and please remember this) when we begin to deal directly with tangents we *almost* give up introducing people to Christ; yet one of these texts by the grace of God may trigger a flicker of understanding. Here are twenty-one of the most popular tangents used.

I Am Already Better Than Most Christians I Know

Obviously a person who tells you that he is better than some Christians he knows is reacting to something you said earlier—either about Christians being better people or about his own sinful condition. Either way, this humanitarian must be made to see *his* sins personally and recognize that *all* have sinned. God does not grade us on the curve—better than, worse than. It's all strictly individualistic.

Let's look at what the Bible says about those who consider themselves only half-bad when compared to others.

> "There is no one righteous, not even one;
>   there is no one who understands,
>   no one who searches for God.
> All have turned away
>   and together become worthless.
> There is no one who does good,
>   not even one."
>
> Rom. 3:10–12

"For all have sinned and fall short of the glory of God" (Rom. 3:23). It isn't necessary to compare ourselves with anyone. Paul said, "A man is not justified by observing the law, but by faith in Jesus Christ" (Gal. 2:16). God does not compare us with each other; it's a personal thing. If we are better than someone else, we can't take any credit for it. "For it is by grace you have been saved, through faith—and this is not from yourselves, it is the gift of God" (Eph. 2:8). Salvation is a gift because no matter how good we are or how much better we are than the next guy we are still just as guilty. God said, "For whoever keeps the whole law, and yet stumbles at just one point, is guilty of breaking all of it" (James 2:10).

You probably just rattled off those verses rapidly in your mind, but when you use these texts in a witnessing experience, allow them time to work. Wait for a reaction before starting a new one. Remember that you are already dealing with the tangent. Your purpose is only to try to salvage what you can. Let the person talk and get it off his chest. After he's had his say, smile kindly and give him the next text from God.

At the conclusion of each selected verse you could zero in again on Jesus Christ, and you should. Even though you know the devil is working in the tangent-seeker, you are still obligated to introduce *Jesus* who alone can defeat him.

People who consider themselves good enough or better than most are only deceiving themselves; rather than arguing with them, ask if they would mind if you thought about their question, prayed about it, researched God's Word on it, and then answered them in a letter. They may even agree to let you do this, especially if you ask in a pleasant way.

This suggestion is not in conflict with what I said earlier (on the seventh rule of witnessing in the last chapter) about pressing for a decision *now* instead of giving a person time to think it over. Why? Because obviously this type of individual is not thinking at all, let alone thinking about a commitment to Christ. It's exciting to harvest fruit, but we shouldn't pick it unless ripe. In this chapter, we are talking about unripened fruit—those who are obviously not yet ready to commit themselves or those who may have actually justified their procrastination in their own minds. The next step is the hardening of their hearts.

In your letter, include texts like: "For it is by grace you have been saved, through faith—and this not from yourselves, it is the gift of God—not of works, so that no one can boast" (Eph. 2:8-9). You may also want to include 1 Corinthians 6:9-11, Matthew 18:3, and Galatians 5:19-21; then if they are ready, also include Galatians 5:22-26, Revelation 21:8, and finally Revelation 22:14-15. These texts are starters; one might add others as they apply to each person.

Nobody Can Know for Sure Whether He's Saved or Not

This ploy robs many of the joy of salvation and allows the victim to divert our witness in order to avoid a direct confrontation with Jesus Christ. He will say, "How can I know for sure that I'm saved until I get there?"

Here are God's answers: "Whoever hears my word and believes him who sent me has eternal life and will not be condemned; he has crossed over [not guilty] from death to life" (John 5:24). Paul told us: "If anyone is in Christ, he is a new creation" (2 Cor. 5:17). In Romans we read: "Those who are led by the Spirit of God are sons of God" (Rom. 8:14). John explained: "If we confess our sins, he is faithful and just and will forgive us our sins and purify us from all unrighteousness" (1 John 1:9); and again: "I write these things to you who believe in the name of the Son of God so that you may know that you have eternal life" (1 John 5:13).

Continued refusal to believe these words is tantamount to denying the truth of Scripture, Christ's full atonement, His death, and the resurrection. When one uses this excuse, he may be very sincere. Some are honestly plagued by doubt, and they require much patience; others use this tangent as an excuse to avoid a decision for Christ. In either case, they are missing the joy of it all and they grieve the Holy Spirit. This stance assumes more knowledge within one's self than trust in God. The pretense may be a fabrication, and if so— as tactfully as possible—lead them to see their façade for what it is. You may also want to share with them John 3:36 and 1 John 2:3.

Let Me Think about It for a While

We concluded earlier that we should not allow someone time to delay his decision. Procrastination should be recognized in the potential believer as a cancer and dealt with as such. Just as there are many forms of cancer, there are many ways to procrastinate. The final excuse usually sounds something like this: "Some other time," "See me tomorrow," "I'm too busy," "I never make major decisions alone," or "I'll have to talk it over at home first."

God answers, "Seek the Lord while he may be found; call on him while he is near. Let the wicked forsake his way and the evil man his thoughts. Let him turn to the Lord, and he will have mercy on him, and to our God, for he will freely pardon" (Isa. 55:6–7). And who can ignore the parable of the rich fool which climaxes in these words: "But God said unto him, 'You fool! This very night your life will be demanded from you. Then who will get what you have prepared for yourself?'" (Luke 12:20). If all else fails, we might want to point out that there just might be no tomorrow: "Boast not thyself of tomorrow; for thou knowest not what a day may bring forth" (Prov. 27:1, kjv). "I tell you,

now is the time of God's favor, now is the day of salvation"
(2 Cor. 6:2). Finally there is the awesome warning from
God Himself that should be passed on to every procrastinator: "He, that being often reproved [witnessed to] hardeneth his neck, shall suddenly be destroyed, and that without remedy" (Prov. 29:1, KJV). And "How shall we escape if
we ignore such a great salvation? This salvation, which was
first announced by the Lord, was confirmed to us by those
who heard him" (Heb. 2:3).

Later you may want to write a letter as we suggested
earlier. You may wish to repeat the texts listed above and
include Proverbs 8:17, Matthew 18:3, and Hebrews 3:13–15
(especially v. 15).

My Sin Is Too Great. Only I Know How Bad I Am.
You Have No Idea.

This tangent is often used by an individual who has been
overly convinced of the terribleness of his sins. He will say,
"Wow, you just don't understand the things I have done;
nobody could forgive all that." This tangent may also be
used by a person harboring a secret sin, one that carries so
much shame and guilt that he knows that God turned His
head in disgust—just as He does for every sin committed.

This awareness does not preclude forgiveness. Here's
God's answer to this self-incriminating soul: "If we confess
our sin, he is faithful and just and will forgive us our sins
and purify us from all unrighteousness" (1 John 1:9). Right
beyond that text is another which better describes the enor-
mity of our Lord's forgiving potential: "If anybody does sin,
we have one who speaks to the Father in our defense—Jesus
Christ, the Righteous One. He is the atoning sacrifice for our

sins, and not only for ours but also for the sins of the whole world" (1 John 2:1–2). How could any single sinner amass a debt so great as to bankrupt that potential? Isn't that a magnificent text for both the witnessee and the witnesser? You might also want to mention Isaiah 1:18: " 'Come now, let us reason together,' says the Lord. 'Though your sins are like scarlet, they shall be as white as snow; though they are red as crimson, they shall be like wool.' " There just may be a little bit of Bible knowledge tucked away in the back of this person's head that could be transferred to his heart. Quote the verse, wait, smile, and pray silently every second, believing that the Holy Spirit is convicting and convincing, not you.

Repenting is the key to the forgiveness of sins; so we should include this text also: "Repent, then, and turn to God, so that your sins may be wiped out" (Acts 3:19). Should you have to write or if the occasion presents itself, you may also want to share the following texts with the person who is oppressed by guilt: Matthew 12:31; Hebrews 10:26, 31; Matthew 18:21–35; Galatians 6:1–5. Then actually pray Psalm 51 with him. This psalm hits the nail right on the head, the nail that pierced Christ's hand and feet, whereby our forgiveness was made sure.

I'm Waiting for the Eleventh Hour

This person understands enough Scripture to know about the thief on the cross who made it during his eleventh hour (Luke 23:43). He forgets, however, that there were two thieves on the cross and that the other didn't make it. He forgets too that he could die in the tenth hour.

God knew some would use the example of the thief on the

cross; so, as if keeping with that theme, He says: "The day of
the Lord will come like a thief in the night. While people are
saying, 'Peace and safety,' destruction will come on them
suddenly, as labor pains on a pregnant woman, and they
will not escape" (1 Thess. 5:2–3). Jesus Himself said, "You
also must be ready, because the Son of Man will come at an
hour when you do not expect him" (Matt. 24:44). Paul said,
"Now [today] is the day of salvation" (2 Cor. 6:2). You
might want to read the account of the ten virgins found in
Matthew 25:1–13; those who didn't make it were called
"foolish" by Jesus Himself. It's all over the very instant one
dies; there's no second chance, no opportunity to do it over
or to do it better. It is finished for eternity. What a hor-
rendous gamble these people are taking. (To help you cope
with this sidetrack, you should also review all of "Let me
think about it for a while," tangent number 3.)

I Believe That If I'm Elect I'll Make It

This tangent-seeker is hanging on to a doctrine instead of
Jesus Christ! "Once saved, always saved!" "If I'm elect, I'll
make it." "If I sin, that must have been in God's plans. I was
predestined to sin these particular sins, so get off my back."
All such statements are fatalistic and carry eternal consequences.

Paul answers, "Do not be deceived: God cannot be
mocked. A man reaps what he sows. The one who sows to
please his sinful nature, from that nature will reap destruction; the one who sows to please the Spirit, from the Spirit
will reap eternal life" (Gal. 6:7–8). "The acts of the sinful
nature are obvious: sexual immorality, impurity and de-
bauchery; idolatry and witchcraft; hatred, discord, jealousy,

fits of rage, selfish ambition, dissensions, factions and envy; drunkenness, orgies, and the like. I warn you, as I did before, that those who live like this will not inherit the kingdom of God" (Gal. 5:19–21).

Confront these tangent-seekers as though Peter, Paul, and Timothy were all standing there each speaking in turn. First Peter would say, "[You may be elect, I don't know, but] Christ suffered for you, leaving you an example, that you should follow in his steps" (1 Pet. 2:21). Paul would chime right in with "You have been set free from sin and have become slaves to righteousness" (Rom. 6:18). "If you live according to the sinful nature, you will die; but if by the Spirit you put to death the misdeeds of the body, you will live. Those who are led by the Spirit of God are sons of God" (Rom. 8:13–14). "For now we really live, since you are standing firm in the Lord" (1 Thess. 3:8). "Do not deceive yourselves. If any one of you thinks that he is wise [in doctrinal tangentitis] by the standards of this age, he should become a 'fool' so that he may become wise" (1 Cor. 3:18). "Don't you know that the wicked will not inherit the kingdom of God? [again I say to you] Do not be deceived" (1 Cor. 6:9). Timothy would quickly add: "If we disown him, he will also disown us" (2 Tim. 2:12). Now Paul would really get excited and caution our brother with these words: "If we deliberately keep on sinning after we have received the knowledge of the truth, no sacrifice for sins is left" (Heb. 10:26).

Hell? You Gotta Be Kidding!

One of the favorite tricks of the devil is to trap us into proving that hell exists instead of talking about Jesus. The person who employs this tangent will usually bring up the subject. If we are beyond the point where we can effectively introduce him to Jesus, then we may want to try to leave him something of what God has to say about hell. God warns us of the eternal life of fire: "And they will go out and look upon the dead bodies of those who rebelled against me; their worm will not die, nor will their fire be quenched, and they will be loathsome to all mankind" (Isa. 66:24). Need it be any more didactic?

Chances are, if this person doesn't believe in hell, he doesn't accept a hereafter of any sort. This may be directly related to the fact that he does not make a practice of reading God's Word. We might want to point him to Christ's story about the rich man and Lazarus (Luke 16:19–31), Christ's words spoken to the thief on the cross: "Today you will be with me in paradise" (Luke 23:43), or Christ's teachings about offenses where He talks plainly about hell (Mark 9:43–49).

Since we become involved in this kind of discussion only because the person we are witnessing to refuses to hear of Jesus and insists on presenting his hang-ups as an alternative to our witness, I mention once more the possibility of writing a follow-up letter. We might include statements that Jesus made concerning the existence of hell: "Do not be afraid of those who kill the body but cannot kill the soul. Rather, be afraid of the one who can destroy both soul and body in hell" (Matt. 10:28). "The Son of Man [Jesus] . . . will weed out [unbelievers] . . . and . . . throw them into the fiery furnace, where there will be weeping and grinding of teeth" (Matt. 13:41–42). Jesus also said, "Then he [God] will say to those on his left [sinners], 'Depart from me, you who are cursed, into the eternal fire prepared for the devil and his angels'" (Matt. 25:41). "Then they [sinners] will go away to eternal punishment, but the righteous to eternal life" (Matt. 25:46). We let Jesus' words describe the existence of hell in the knowledge, assurance, and faith that His Word will not return void.

God Is Dead or Jesus Was a Good Guy
Who Got Himself Hanged

It's hard to believe, but there are those who would stop you on the second word of John 3:16: "For God so loved . . ." They don't understand who God really is, and so they say, "For who?" After a short pause they may add, "What God?" Their "god" could well be that which comes from a high on drugs, or "the force that puts it all together," or something even more nauseous to a committed Christian. Just swallow hard and remember that many didn't know who Jesus was when He stood right in front of them.

We present God to as many varied backgrounds and twisted concepts as there are unbelievers. The power of answered prayer as your proof that God is alive and well won't mean a thing to this breed of tangent-seeker. Nevertheless, God is alive, and their denial of that fact will not make God go away or die. God will judge that person just as surely as He will judge the whole world.

Let's deal with this force that puts it all together. The Bible says, "For since the creation of the world God's invisible qualities—his eternal power and divine nature—have been clearly seen, being understood from what has been made, so that men are without excuse. For although they knew God, they neither glorified him as God" (Rom. 1:20–21). "In the beginning God" (Gen. 1:1, KJV). "In the beginning . . . all things were made; without him nothing was made that has been made" (John 1:1–3). God is alive, and He is seen in general revelation, in His creation, and also in His Son.

By now we have left the witness to follow the tangent. This is about as far as we should go at this point. Follow up by a letter which includes such texts as John 3:18 and Mark 16:16.

However, if the person we are talking to agrees that Jesus was a real person—even though He, in their opinion, was only a nice guy—then we have some more work to do before we trot off to write a letter. Those who feel Jesus was just a good guy but is now dead obviously have no regard for the atonement or Christ's deity. They wouldn't understand either of these terms anyway. What's more, most texts that deal with Christ's day-by-day life occur in the New Testament, whereas, it might be better for this person if we referred more to Old Testament passages. Point them to the story of the Passover; read them Isaiah 53 and the other verses that were pointed to previously in chapter 9.

Those who disregard the atonement and Christ's deity should be prayerfully made aware of texts like Isaiah 9:6–7 and Micah 5:1–2. Then ask them to read Matthew 1:19–25 with you slowly, word-by-word and thought-by-thought, pausing long enough to allow for questions. (We are side-tracked anyway.)

If we finally must resort to a follow-up letter, include other texts such as John 1:1, 14, 5:19–23; Philippians 2:5–11; Colossians 1:15–19, 2:9–15; Hebrews 1:1–8; and 1 John 5:7–9.

How Can I Believe What I Cannot Understand?

This unbeliever tries to sell you his logic while admitting that he lacks ability to understand. Obviously he is easier to deal with because there are so many things that none of us understand in this world yet we place our faith in them. For example, a jet weighing tons will lift off the ground and stay in the air for thousands of miles. We believe that from the ground. When we board it for a trip, we demonstrate our faith in it; yet few understand the physics behind it all. The same is true of spiritual matters. Paul said, "The man without the Spirit does not accept the things that come from the Spirit of God, for they are foolishness to him, and he cannot understand them, because they are spiritually discerned. The spiritual man makes judgments about all things, but he himself is not subject to any man's judgment: 'For who has known the mind of the Lord that he may instruct him?' But, we have the mind of Christ" (1 Cor. 2:14–16). A strong statement of reassurance is imperative. We need not fully comprehend in order to believe; however, another word of caution from Paul is also necessary: "The god [devil] of this age has blinded the minds of unbelievers, so that they cannot see the light of the gospel of the glory of Christ, who is the image of God" (2 Cor. 4:4).

Offer to pray for wisdom and understanding with him now before it is too late. God said, "Incline thine ear unto wisdom, and apply thy heart to understanding" (Prov. 2:2, KJV). From where does this wisdom and understanding come? "For the Lord giveth wisdom: out of his mouth [the Word] cometh knowledge and understanding" (Prov. 2:6, KJV). "Happy is the man that findeth wisdom, and the man that getteth understanding" (Prov. 3:13). "Wisdom is the principal thing; therefore get wisdom: and with all thy getting, get understanding" (Prov. 4:7).

You might also want to direct his attention to Proverbs 24:7, Ecclesiastes 2:13, and Job 28:28. Then show him how to get wisdom: "If any of you lacks wisdom, he should ask God, who gives generously to all without finding fault, and it will be given to him" (James 1:5). Offer once more to pray with him. Don't write to this one. He's too close. Grab him now. Reread the words of Paul in 2 Corinthians 4:4.

I Don't Want to Be a Churchgoing Hypocrite

We dealt with part of this excuse earlier; however, in this case it might be well to agree that there are hypocrites in the visible church but that the visible church will not go to heaven or hell. As individuals, we are judged before God. Usually about the last of all excuses is the failings of the visible church. Press on now for the commitment and promise to return later to answer that question. Once one has given himself to the Lord, his prior question has little continuing significance.

Should the witnessee absolutely insist on being sidetracked by the question of the visible church, offer him Jesus *without* the visible church by pointing out that the visible church does not save. Use the thief on the cross as an example. Do not write this person either. He's ready now. Release him from the power of his pseudo-hang-up (the church) by offering him the living Savior. Once a person accepts the Person of Jesus Christ through the indwelling of the Holy Spirit, he will automatically also accept the church because the church is the "Body of Christ" (Rom. 12:5; 1 Cor. 12:27; Eph. 1:22–23, 4:12; Col. 1:24, 2:19).

If the church is the Body of Christ, it stands to reason that Christ should be the Head of the church (Eph. 1:22, 4:15, 5:23; Col. 1:18, 2:19). Christ the Head of the church is also pictured in Scripture as the Bridegroom of the church (Matt. 9:15, 25:1–6; John 3:29; Rev. 21:2), and we are the bride (Isa. 62:5; 2 Cor. 11:2; Rev. 19:7, 21:2, 22:17) in holy union with one another and with our Lord (Rom. 7:4; 1 Cor. 6:15; 2 Cor. 11:2; Eph. 5:30; 1 John 2:24), forming the family of God (Deut. 14:2; Isa. 63:16; Hos. 11:1; John 1:12; Rom. 8:15–16; 2 Cor. 6:18; Gal. 4:5–6).

I Don't Believe the Bible Is True

No more difficult tangent exists. Without the Bible as your witnessing tool, you have no weapon at all. The devil is happily aware of this fact. How do we proceed with someone who from the outset wants to declare that the ground rules for any discussion eliminate our use of Scripture? His reasons are not really important, and they will range all the way from a claim that the Bible is not totally accurate to the claim that it is nothing more than a storybook.

We should compliment this person for having studied the Scripture so well as to be able to warrant conclusions about it. Then ask him what, in his opinion, is the central teaching of the Word. When he hems and haws and realizes he doesn't know, we can answer the question ourselves by getting right back to the subject of Jesus Christ. If this doesn't work, we must repair the disbelief by proving the authenticity of the Scriptures. Impossible task? No. Here are a few things on which to concentrate while praying that the Holy Spirit will work a miracle.

In addition to what was already covered in chapter 9, here are two more verses one might consider from Scripture. (I say "from Scripture" because only Scripture is going to prove itself true, not you or I.) "All scripture is given by inspiration of God, and is profitable for doctrine, for reproof, for correction, for instruction in righteousness: That the man of God may be perfect, thoroughly furnished unto all good works" (2 Tim. 3:16–17, KJV). Stop, let it sink in, repeat it, and then go on to this verse: "For prophecy never had its origin in the will of man, but men spoke from God as they were carried along by the Holy Spirit" (2 Pet. 1:21). Let that sink in also. Repeat it if necessary.

Some tangent-lovers sincerely feel that Scripture cannot be God's infallible Word because it leaves too much unsaid. They reason that if God really wrote it He would have told us more. "God is perfect," they say, "therefore, He'd have done a perfect job of telling us several things that your Bible omits." This individual has probably read the Bible before and may even be a student of the Scriptures, but he probably forgot what God tells us in Deuteronomy: "The secret things belong unto the Lord our God: but those things which are revealed belong unto us and to our children for ever, that we may do all the words of this law [Bible]" (Deut. 29:29, KJV).

Then there are those who have another excuse for not believing that the Bible is the holy and infallible Word of God. They say, "The Bible is poetry." They're right. It is also history. It is a collection of proverbial sayings, laws, parables, hymns, riddles, letters, allegories, prophecy, drama, and good literature. It is all this and more. It is the inspired Word of God, covering every known manner of literary style and human expression. It was written at different times by forty men. It contains prophecies that have been fulfilled and more that are being fulfilled now. It is a best seller today and has been on the market for hundreds of years.

Some more interesting facts about Scripture might well be pointed out at this time since we are now dealing with the tangent itself. The Bible itself claims to be inspired by God in 2 Timothy 3:16. The Bible was given to us by various means: some of it came directly from God's mouth via His voice (Exod. 19:19; Matt. 3:17; John 12:28); other portions were given by the angels (Acts 7:38–40; Heb. 2:2), the prophets, Jesus Himself, and five apostles; and all kinds of visions, dreams, and revelations make up the Bible.

Before we try to prove the Bible true or even use it in witnessing, we had better know it in depth. We attribute many things to the Bible that aren't true because they aren't there! As important as it is to know what is contained in Scriptures, one should also be aware of a few popular quotations that are often passed off as scriptural but are not. "Money is the root of all evil" is not in the Bible. "The *love* of . . ." *is* in Scripture. "Charity begins at home" is not in the Bible. "Cleanliness is next to godliness" is not in the Bible. "It is better to cast your seed in the belly of a whore than to spill it on the ground" is not in the Bible. "Spare the rod and spoil the child" is not in the Bible in *those* words. "God helps those who help themselves" is not in the Bible. "God tempers the wind for the shorn lamb" is not in the Bible. We must be very careful not to nod approval of a so-called biblical quotation which we are not sure is in the Bible, especially if the person quoting it doesn't believe the Bible is inspired.

None Will Perish. Everyone Will Be Saved. God Is Love.

It was difficult enough to deal with the man who refused assurance of salvation, stating he wasn't confident he was saved; but here's another tangent—the man who believes that *everyone* will be saved.

God's answer to him is very direct. Jesus said, "Enter through the narrow gate. For wide is the gate and broad is the road that leads to destruction, and many enter through it. But small is the gate and narrow is the road that leads to life, and only a few find it" (Matt. 7:13–14). Not everyone will be saved! Paul added, "Don't you know that the wicked will not inherit the kingdom of God?" (1 Cor. 6:9).

It's hard for the born-again Christian to understand how anyone could really believe in salvation for all because the Scriptures tell us differently. Just as easily, others believe anything they want to because they are not reading the Scriptures. Therefore, we have all the more reason to introduce them to the truth. God said, "But the . . . unbelieving . . . their place will be in the fiery lake of burning sulfur" (Rev. 21:8). Jesus said, "Whoever believes in him [Jesus Christ] is not condemned, but whoever does not believe stands condemned already because he has not believed in the name of God's one and only Son" (John 3:18). One should exercise caution in differentiating clearly between historic and saving faith as we spelled out in our chapter on faith.

I have some difficulty picturing the value of writing a follow-up letter to this tangent-seeker; however, should it become necessary, you might want to share Mark 16:16, Galatians 5:19–21, Psalm 9:17, and Revelation 21:8.

Don't Get So Uptight. We'll All Get Another Crack at It.

This wise guy believes he will have another chance after death, so why shape up now? Actually such a person not only misses the boat but is also totally incapable of sensing the joy of being on board in Christ. Paul would blow his mind once and for all with these words: "Man is destined to die once, and after that to face judgment" (Heb. 9:27)!

Chances are, you won't get far with this self-proclaimed genius; so you will probably have to write him a follow-up letter. You might want to share this verse: "He, that being often reproved [as you are now doing] [soon] hardeneth his neck, [and] shall suddenly be destroyed, and that without remedy" (Prov. 29:1, KJV). Also consider Revelation 21:8, 22:14–16.

I'm Not Good Enough Yet. Give Me Time.

Have you ever met the superhonest, dallying tangent-seeker who says, "I'm not good enough for God," or "not good enough for church," or "not good enough to be a Christian"? Here's God's answer to him. " 'Come now, let us reason together,' says the Lord. 'Though your sins are like scarlet, they shall be as white as snow; though they are red as crimson, they shall be as wool' " (Isa. 1:18). Remembering that we are already on a tangent, dwell on the word *while* found in Isaiah 55:6–7 in one more attempt to return to the Person of Christ. If this doesn't take hold, read what Isaiah said: "All of us have become like one who is unclean, and all our righteousness is like filthy rags; we all shrivel up like a leaf, and like the wind our sins sweep us away. . . . Yet, O Lord, you are our Father. We are the clay, you are the potter; we are all the work of your hand" (Isa. 64:6, 8).

An important consideration to bear in mind when someone tells you that he is not good enough for God is that this person has taken the first step toward realizing he needs a Savior. This is a good start if he's sincere (which often isn't the case). If he insists on following his line of reasoning instead of making the commitment, use this additional text about his so-called unworthiness: "He [God] saved us, not because of righteous things we had done, but because of his mercy. He saved us through the washing of rebirth and renewal by the Holy Spirit, whom he poured out on us generously through Jesus Christ our Savior, so that, having been justified by his grace, we might become heirs having the hope of eternal life" (Tit. 3:5–7).

Paul said it another way: "For it is by grace you have been saved [not by being worthy yourselves], through faith —and this not from yourselves, it is the gift of God—not by works, so that no one can boast" (Eph. 2:8–9). Of course, 1 John 1:9 shouldn't be forgotten for just such an occasion as this: "If we confess our sins, he is faithful and just and will forgive us our sins and purify us from all unrighteousness."

This sinner is pathetic. He may be screaming to you for assurances. He might be hoping in his heart—behind the façade—that you will persist and break through. His argumentation might be a secret invitation to press on. If there is the least glimmer of hope, reach out and grab hold. Be firm about the necessity of decision. Often, after an individual accepts Christ, he breaks down, confessing that all along he knew this had to occur and now is thankful it has happened. Don't be timid. Break this person away from Satan's grip.

Introduce Jesus once again in love. Ask him to accept Jesus right now in a simple prayer. Make up one for him on the spot. God knows what's going on, and our feeble efforts won't offend Him if we are honestly trying to help someone see Jesus Christ. God knows that we are only the cracked vessels described in Psalm 31:12; yet He works through us.

I Don't Want to Give Up Everything

This superhonest swinger says, "There are just too many things that I'd have to give up, and I know too many hypocrites who call themselves Christians already. When I become a Christian, I'll be a good one; but I'm not ready yet! I can't force myself to give up this or that, and I don't want to even if I could!"

Here's God's answer: "Set your minds on things above, not on earthly things" (Col. 3:2). This tangent-seeker would love to have you get off his back about Jesus and negotiate a compromise. Suppose he or she is living out of wedlock and knows this sin will have to go if Jesus comes into his or her heart. "Can't we negotiate this situation?" he'll be asking, probably unashamedly. The sin may be drugs, alcohol, or another love. Here's God's answer to every covetous sin: "Love the Lord your God with all your heart, with all your soul, with all your mind and with all your strength" (Mark 12:30). There is no compromise.

If the swinger sincerely wishes to give up those things which God declares sinful, then God promises victory: "No temptation has seized you except what is common to man. And God is faithful; he will not let you be tempted beyond what you can bear. But when you are tempted, he will also provide a way out so that you can stand up under it" (1 Cor. 10:13).

The problem may be much shallower; perhaps the concern is just pure selfishness. "I'm having a ball, and I don't intend to exchange it for a stick-in-the-mud religious kick." Assure him that Jesus Christ doesn't represent giving up anything. He is a whole new life of real joy, not just one who provides kicks here and there.

God doesn't suggest that this frolic-seeker give up his lark;

He commands him to do it or perish. He also promises to give him the grace to say no to sin. "For the grace of God that brings salvation has appeared to all men. It teaches us to say 'No' to ungodliness and worldly passions, and to live self-controlled, upright and godly lives in this present age" (Tit. 2:11–12).

The person who uses this tangent has his priorities upside down. God would carry the point one step further. Suppose you could have what you won't give up and even more. God now asks: "What good will it be for a man if he gains the whole world, yet forfeits his soul? Or what can a man give in exchange for his soul?" (Matt. 16:26). Are these fun and games worth the consequences of hell?

Pursue the subject of heaven. Ask him why God would let him in? What if the pleasures he clings to were the very thing that caused God to say, "I never knew you, [use his full name]." Assure him that God will help him (1 John 1:9; 1 Cor. 10:13). Then reestablish the truth that the only reason anyone gains entrance into heaven is Christ's merits through our total surrender to His substitutionary act of atonement.

I Just Can't Live a Good Enough Life

The next tangent-seeker says, "I have tried to live a good life, and I can't. I am just too weak to live by all those standards. You don't understand me."

Here's God's answer: "You, dear children, are from God and have overcome them [these hassles and weaknesses]" (1 John 4:4).

No doubt his first response will be, "I tried that, but it didn't work." As long as we are off on the tangent anyway, ask him if he has *really* tried. Of course the answer will be an impatient yes. He is now set up for the next question: "Did you try it alone, or did you ask God to do it for you?" Wait for an answer. Let him commit himself one way or the other so that you will know how to follow through.

If he tried to go it alone, then we would want to implant these texts in his mind and heart: "Do not be deceived: God cannot be mocked. A man reaps what he sows" (Gal. 6:7). James addressed these words to those who attempt to succeed by themselves: "Submit yourselves, then come to God. Resist the devil, and he will flee from you" (James 4:7). No doubt it *is* tough to go it alone. Proverbs agrees that "the way of trangressors is hard" (Prov. 13:15, KJV) because the wrong-doer's way includes the aftermath as well.

If, on the other hand, the witnessee says he has asked God to help but nothing happened, then we've tricked him a little by using the word *ask* instead of the word *trust* in our question. We should explain what *trust* is, in addition to what *asking* is all about. Jesus said, "Come to me, all you [go-it-aloners] who are weary and burdened, and I [Jesus] will give you rest. Take my yoke upon you and learn from me, for I am gentle and humble in heart, and you will find rest for your souls. For my yoke is easy and my burden is light" (Matt. 11:28–30).

When we go it alone, we fail. The Bible tells us that Christ "is able to keep you from falling" (Jude 24); "Jesus . . . will save his people" (Matt. 1:21); "You will keep in perfect peace him whose mind is steadfast because he trusts in you" (Isa. 26:3). Finally, Paul said, "God is able to make all grace abound to you, so that in all things at all times, having all that you need, you will abound in every good work" (2 Cor. 9:8). You may also wish to share 1 Corinthians 10:13 with this tangent-seeker. In any case, include Psalm 103:14: "For he knoweth our frame; he remembereth that we are dust" (KJV). Emphasize the fact that God has provided for the forgiveness of our failure through Jesus Christ.

God Is Too Good to Damn Anyone

This tangent might first appear similar to two earlier ones: "There is no hell," and "None will perish; everyone will be saved." However, this one misrepresents God's personality as well as His justice. The texts to refer to will, therefore, be different also.

Here's what God would have us say, using His holy Word: "Whoever does not believe will be condemned" (Mark 16:16). Jesus Himself said, "Not everyone who says to me, 'Lord, Lord,' will enter the kingdom of heaven" (Matt. 7:21). Jesus also said, "But unless you repent, you too will all perish" (Luke 13:5). You might also like to share Proverbs 1:22–23 in this case.

Aw, It's Just Got to Be Harder Than That to Get Saved. This Is Too Easy.

It wasn't easy for Jesus Christ! It has been made easier for us. It might be well to review John 3:16–22, Ephesians 2:8–9, and Acts 3:19 and then invite this person to trust God's promises. "It was not through law that Abraham and his offspring received the promise that he would be the heir of the world, but through the righteousness that comes by faith" (Rom. 4:13). Paul stated, "And you also were included in Christ when you heard the word of the truth, the gospel of your salvation. In him, when you believed, you were marked with a seal, the promised Holy Spirit" (Eph.

1:13). "Do not grieve the Holy Spirit of God" (Eph. 4:30) by procrastinating another hour. It might also be a good idea to review the section on discipleship (chap. 11) as another proof that salvation and the Christian life are not easy.

Hey, Look. God Will Save Me When He Gets Ready. Okay?

He is ready and has been from eternity. Jesus said, "The time has come, . . . The kingdom of God is near. Repent and believe the good news!" (Mark 1:15).

The witnessee might well respond, "Okay, that's in the Bible, written hundreds of years ago, but I'm here today. How does all that old stuff apply to me?" Paul answered, "God our Savior . . . wants all men to be saved and to come to a knowledge of the truth [Christ]" (1 Tim. 2:3–4). Pause for a moment; then let Peter nail it down with these words: "The Lord is not slow in keeping his promise, as some understand slowness. He is patient with you, not wanting anyone to perish, but everyone to come to repentance. But the day of the Lord will come like a thief" (2 Pet. 3:9–10). Repentance leads to 1 John 1:9, and one would hope to a prayer of commitment.

Point out to this person that God is ready right now, otherwise His Holy Spirit would not have bothered setting up this witness today. God uses people to bring other people His word: "Now is the accepted time; behold, now is the day of salvation" (2 Cor. 6:2, kjv). Also read Isaiah 55:6–7 to him.

Hey, I Am All Right. I Vote, Help the Community Drive, and Don't Beat My Wife.

He may even add, "What more do you want?" This would allow a perfect opportunity for saying, "It's not what I or your community or even your wife wants; it is what God wants, and He wants you."

God said, "The promise is for you and your children and for all who are far off—for all whom the Lord our God will call" (Acts 2:39). No matter how good we are toward our country or family, no matter how much we do for God, no matter what we accomplish for the church, God still says, "All of us have become like one who is unclean, and all our righteousness is like filthy rags; we all shrivel up like a leaf, and like the wind our sins sweep us away" (Isa. 64:6).

No matter how admirable one may seem in someone else's eyes (and helping with community affairs is good), good works do not save us (see Eph. 2:8–9). The Bible says:

"There is no one righteous, not even one;
   there is no one who understands,
   no one who searches for God.
All have turned away
   and together become worthless.
There is no one who does good,
   not even one."

                    Rom. 3:10–12

"For all have sinned and fall short of the glory of God" (Rom. 3:23). None of us—no matter who we are or what we've done—is worthy of God's attention, care, love, pardon, grace, forgiveness, or the gift of eternal life until we see our unworthiness and seek the righteousness of Jesus Christ, our Redeemer. (Read 2 Cor. 5:21.)

Dwell on the word Redeemer. In most dictionaries, one of the definitions is "Jesus Christ"! After the act of redemption is fully explained, then apply this text: "Repent, then, and turn to God, so that your sins may be wiped out" (Acts 3:19). Explain that it is through Christ's righteousness alone that we obtain heaven.

God Is Unfair. What about the Poor People Who Never Heard? Why Should They Go to Hell?

Who's judging whom? Obviously, this person has no sensitivity to man's unworthiness. Instead of looking at the matter his way, attempt to turn things around the way Scripture presents the issue. All of us deserve hell. When God sees our sin, He judges us worthy of hell—all of us. But when God sees us through Jesus Christ—who took away all our sins (past, present, and future)—He sees us as perfect and judges us worthy of heaven.

Beginning with the fact that all men deserve hell, this tangent-seeker can see that God is gracious, instead of unfair, when He saves some through His Son's death and paid-up penalty. This is God's plan of salvation which you are transmitting to him at this very moment. It's an individual and personal matter. Encourage him to see it in that light.

Share with this person Romans 3:23, 6:23; Ephesians 2:8–9; Titus 3:5; Proverbs 14:12; Isaiah 53:4; and John 3:16–17. He has drawn a man-made conclusion which is not based on Scripture.

There are probably a million more excuses that people who are running away from our Lord will use to justify themselves. Just as soon as we uncover one of them and answer it, the devil will supply another. More texts could have been included for the answer to each tangent; however, additional verses will come to your mind from the Spirit's work in you as you actually witness for Christ. Be reassured that every witness is a successful experience in God's sight. No witness fails when performed in His will, strength, purpose, and plan.

In no way do I consider myself an expert on witnessing. I have personally grieved the Holy Spirit more often than I have obeyed His impulse to implant, but, praise God, He forgave and continues to want to use even me.

Speaking to others about Jesus Christ is exciting, regardless of the immediate results or "lack" of results. However, after the person you witness to makes a commitment to Christ the real work begins—the follow-up. When God gives you the honor and thrill of bringing another to Him, He also gives you the responsibility of caring for this new babe in Christ. Follow-up is a complex subject that is best understood as growth in the Lord. Naturally some will "plant," others will "water," and still others will "reap"; but those who reap must also keep. Always follow up.

14

The Follow-up

The most important decision anyone ever makes between birth and death is to personally accept or reject Jesus Christ as Savior and Lord. When one accepts Christ, this decision warrants a follow-up—a deepening exposure to Christ and the Scriptures.

Many follow-up questions will be asked by the new convert, inquiries with a wide range of answers covering a multitude of subjects (including some we already covered in chap. 7). We will attempt to cover most of the other questions throughout the balance of this book. Rather than confuse you, let me outline how we will accomplish this.

First, we are going to search out a deeper Christ. We'll be looking at the nine manifestations of the fruit of His spirit and comparing those to ours in an effort to deepen the faith of the new convert. (We already did something similar with faith in chap. 5.)

Second, we will consider prayer: our prayer life and the prayer life of the new Christian, some reasons for unanswered prayer, how to pray in His will, conditions for answered prayer, reasons for delays in answered prayer, and when to quit praying.

Third, we will attempt to establish the relevancy of Jesus Christ for today by looking at His physical setting in His day. From that perspective we'll see how He still relates two thousand years later. Then finally, we'll wrap it up with a chapter on balance—the theme of God's Word.

Let's begin our follow-up by looking at Christ's inner spirit, the fruit of His spirit, and see how that compares to ours. Christ's spirit is so different from ours that the Bible tells us that when a man is in Christ *he* becomes a new creation (2 Cor. 5:17). So exciting and unique are these new (and often strange, at first) traits in the Christian that they dazzle normal human behavior. They've amazed a few scientists too because God (Christ) is love and Christians exude love as a culmination of all the manifestations of His spirit.

The Seed of Christ's Spirit Is Love

Love is that quality of our Lord's spirit which, if passed through a prism (as a beam of light), would burst forth as a beautiful rainbow of patience, goodness, selflessness, meekness, temperance, unselfishness, peace, purity, joy, gentleness, faith, and hope. But it all begins with love.

The Bible says, "Love is patient [patience], love is kind [goodness]. It does not envy [selfless], it does not boast, it is not proud [meekness]. It is not rude [temperance], it is not self-seeking [unselfish], it is not easily angered [peace], it keeps no record of wrongs [pure]. Love does not delight in evil but rejoices in the truth [joy]. It always protects [gentleness], always trusts [faith], always hopes [hope], always perseveres [endures with longsuffering]" (1 Cor. 13:4–7).

Love, however, is a two-way street. In His love for us, Christ is jealous. He's not about to play second fiddle to sin idols. Do you blame Him? He laid down His life for us (1 John 3:16) and now demands our total love (Matt. 22:37), loyalty, devotion, our every thought, concern, plan, gift, and promise (1 John 3:16–18) in return. He's given us far more (John 15:13). Once He "buys" us, which was from the beginning of time (Matt. 25:34), it's a matter of His loving us through the rest of our life! Love is the most obvious and the most overlooked gift of God. How can this be?

Christ's love for us is so personal that it begins during our prenatal life (Ps. 22:9) and carries through our infancy (Luke 18:15–17) into adolescence (Matt. 19:14) and into adulthood. It follows us into our retirement years and is present during our call back (John 10:1–6) into eternal life (John 3:15).

Every day our Lord earnestly seeks something from each of His children: awareness. He patiently waits for us to grow more spiritually aware. He measures our reactions against those of His own human personality. He patiently waits for our first flicker of growth to indicate to Him (even though He knows our hearts) and to the world around us that we recognize Him as the lover of our souls. He waits for us to begin—even in a simple way—to return His kind of affection.

What is His love like? It's really quite indescribable because in every way it surpasses man's fondest hopes. Paul wanted those at Ephesus to realize "how wide and long and high and deep is the love of Christ, and to know this love that surpasses knowledge" (Eph. 3:18–19). Christ's love never fails; it is always faithful, unchangeable, warm, tender, understanding, patient, kind, intercessary, unselfish, self-sacrificing, loyal, respectful, sincere, constraining, and, most important of all, eternal! It knows no bounds, is not rational, and came to us without our being aware of its coming "while we were yet sinners." Christ's love sticks no matter what and goes beyond temporal loves of family and friends; even a mother's love shrinks in comparison to Christ's love for us (Isa. 49:15; Heb. 13:8; Rom. 8:35–39).

Once He said what so many suitors say, "I love you so much, I would die for you," but *He* meant it and He did it (John 15:13). Now He wants to know just one thing: When will you fully realize it (John 15:9) and act like it (Gal. 2:20; 1 John 3:18) so that others will see Me in you?

How Does Our Love Compare with His

By nature (the old man) we are prone to hate God and our neighbor; yet the hallmark of the committed, spirit-filled Christian is not hate but love. Christ said, "All men will know that you are my disciples if you love one another" (John 13:53)! Do we?

Most of us by nature instinctively strike back when attacked, but the hallmark of a Christian is to turn the other cheek. How? In love, as Christ Himself showed us.

Even the mature Christian has difficulty recognizing Christ's passion at times, and the obvious reason for this is that we don't always experience love or practice it in our daily living. How many of us can honestly claim that we patiently wait our turn in love? How many forgive seventy times seven with longsuffering? How many give from the heart without wanting some recognition or public reward? How many have ever adopted an unpopular person as friend because of "what you do to the least of these . . ."? How many can say we still care when others have all but forgotten? How many can show real humility in the face of success? How many routinely demonstrate compassion instead of self-righteousness when someone slips and stumbles in sin? Jesus did all of this. If we genuinely want to experience Christ's love in our lives, we must start practicing it before we "teach" others to do so.

Christ's Spirit Contains Joy

Our Lord became joy for each of us (of all places) on the cross! Paul said, "Who for the joy set before him endured the cross" (Heb. 12:2). Now, after a personal conversion, we become that joy; we become the sheep on the shepherd's shoulder, and we are the reason for *eternal* joy in heaven. There are two kinds of joy—eternal and temporal. We must be mindful of the extent to which the new convert understands these terms.

Jesus also brought temporal joy to those around Him. His time to work miracles had not yet come. Having just returned from a forty-day hassle with every conceivable temptation Satan could find and refusing to use His supernatural powers to help Himself, at the suggestion of His mother He decided to make others happy. He changed about 150 gallons of water into the most superb wine known to men—His *first* miracle. It is especially noteworthy because "He thus revealed his glory," the power of the Holy Spirit received at His baptism (John 2:11). His subsequent miracles were for the most part performed to relieve suffering; this first one was for festive joy.

If you really want to see delight in our Lord's spirit, look in the mirror! You, the ransomed and redeemed of the Lord, are His living joy today!

How Does Our Joy Compare with His?

Most of us lack the fullest potential of Christ's joy. We
tend to lose our zeal and enthusiasm after maturing from the
new birth. This isn't good or right, but it happens nonetheless. When the new Christian's enthusiasm is high, keep it
there by a renewing of your spirit. We can only experience
His joy by being filled with His Spirit and by energetically
reading and studying His holy Word. It was written "to
make our joy complete" (1 John 1:4).

Christ's Spirit Contains Peace

In our efforts to follow up and deepen an understanding of
the mysteries of God's love, we would also point to that
aspect of His love manifested in His peace. The Bible tells us
that Jesus was "not easily provoked" (1 Cor. 13). Think of
the awful pain, the tearing muscles, the skin and vessels
exploding, the sweat, the utter physical humiliation, and the
unmatched spiritual humiliation that our Lord suffered on
the cross. Added to this agony was the mockery, cursing,
spitting, teasing, heckling, jeering, and mimicking that His
enemies forced Him to bear. He bore it all in peace. While
everything was going on, Jesus asked forgiveness for those
who were crucifying Him.

This same peace, gained for us on the cross (Col. 1:20–
22), is available to new and mature Christians alike. In
times of turmoil, doubt, and temptation, we need only ask
for that peace from the Prince of Peace (Isa. 9:6). He tells
us: "I have told you these things, so that in me you may have
peace. In this world you will have trouble. But take heart! I

have overcome the world" (John 16:33). He's our tranquillity, but only a few experience it long enough to notice.

How Does Our Peace Compare with His?

We go to the world to find "peace" only to be disillusioned. Jesus said, "My peace I give you. I do not give to you as the world gives. Do not let your hearts be troubled and do not be afraid" (John 14:27). Why do mature Christians go running off in the opposite direction to find emptiness? It's important to point out to the new Christian the failures in the lives of even mature Christians. We've already considered some of these failure areas in chapter 7, but let's further recognize that our failure to possess His peace is wrapped up in the fact that we either don't listen to Jesus or we don't believe Him. God's Word plainly tells us that no peace exists for the wicked or for the worldly (Isa. 49:22). God said, "Destruction cometh; and they shall seek peace, and there shall be none" (Ezek. 7:25, KJV); yet many of us continue to search the world for peace because we lack patience. We want it now, even if it is temporal.

Christ's Spirit Contains Patience

The Bible tells us that love "is patient" (1 Cor. 13). Patience is just like every other aspect of the fruit of His Spirit. It was evident in our Lord's encounter with Pontius Pilate and as He endured the cross (Matt. 27:11-28; Mark 15:11-15; John 18:28-40). Patience was also shown to the very young. Remember the little rascals who came running to Jesus during the busyness and heat of the day? (They probably had dirty hands and runny noses.) The Bible tells us that the disciples shooed them away but Jesus showed patience. He took time for them and made a statement we cherish until now: "Let the little children come to me, and do not hinder them, for the kingdom of God belongs to such as these" (Luke 18:16).

Jesus continues to be patient with adult rascals (sinners) today. He calls each of us to repentance and then patiently waits for our response. When you ponder the depth of His free salvation and then consider our procrastination in seeking forgiveness, you can appreciate a little more the endurance of His perfect patience. In your follow-up work allow the new convert to appreciate fully Christ's patience.

Christians, new and mature, fail Him again and again. Many are reluctant to give Him a total commitment. We become blatant, stubborn, proud, and self-seeking. We deny Him while sinning openly and willingly. Even *yet* He is patient enough when we finally confess our sins to forgive and forgive
    and forgive
        and forgive
           and forgive
              and forgive
                and forgive
                  and forgive
                    and forgive
                      and forgive
                        and forgive
                          and forgive.

How Does Our Patience Compare with His?

Patience of any description takes an awful lot of pruning to show even a bud of promise. Patience does not come to us as a prewrapped, sugar-coated gift of the Spirit. It often develops from much sour tribulation and pungent strife. Peter said, "And the God of all grace, who called you to his eternal glory in Christ, after you have suffered a little while, will himself restore you and make you strong, firm and steadfast. To him be the power for ever and ever" (1 Pet. 5:10–11). Suffering often involves tribulations, but thank God for them because without pruning there would be no fruit. Without fruit the branch will be cut off and thrown into the fire as a fruitless waste!

Patience develops through years of growth in the Lord and through years of testing. In his letter to Titus, Paul instructed old men and old women, young men and young women, and servants to possess various qualities, but only the old were expected to show endurance or patience (Tit. 2:2). Don't expect the new convert to mature overnight.

At first glance it appears as though patience might be equated with a good beating and that God will stand over each of us, whipping us with all sorts of problems until we produce patience. Not so. Patience might better be equated to God, in love, force-feeding us something like cod-liver oil to keep us healthy. We may not appreciate the taste or the fact that He has to hold our nose shut to feed it to us, but it's good for us nonetheless! Be sure the new Christian understands that the Christian life is not a "bed of roses"!

James told us, as our parents told us about the cod-liver oil, that often good things come in disguise. Job, of all people, said, "Happy is the man whom God correcteth" (Job 5:17, KJV), and you and I both know that Job realized what he was talking about. James told us, "Count it all joy when ye fall into divers temptations; Knowing this, that the trying of your faith worketh patience" (James 1:2–3, KJV). Like the cod-liver oil, however, it seems so unnecessary to possess, let alone develop.

If one is always in a hurry and if the only way to develop patience is through trials and/or temptations, who needs it? But Paul told us that without patience there is no salvation (Rom. 8:24–25). Now what? Jesus Christ has patience fully developed for us! We must substitute ourselves for Him. We cannot acquire patience without acquiring Him. Scripture tells us that patience is salvation (2 Pet. 3:15) and that we had better begin looking for this perfect endurance in God's Son and not in ourselves. It's all found in our Lord's substitution for us. "For by grace are you saved . . . not of works."

Christ's Spirit also Contains Gentleness, Goodness, Meekness, and Friendship

An example of our Lord's gentleness and understanding was the way he handled the adulteress. Those found guilty of adultery in Jesus' day were stoned. The scribes and Pharisees came dragging the adulteress into the temple where Jesus was sitting, teaching the people. They broke through the crowd, probably interrupting our Lord, plunked her down in the middle of everything, and announced that she was taken in the very act. Jesus just "bent down and started to write on the ground with his finger" as though he never heard them. They persisted: "They kept on questioning him, [until] he straightened up and said to them, 'If any one of you is without sin, let him begin stoning her.' Again he stooped down and wrote on the ground" (John 8:7–8).

The silence must have been unbearable. Then the first shuffle of sandals was heard across the sand courtyard as an old man began to walk away, then another, and soon more— from "the older ones first, until only Jesus was left with the woman still standing there" (v. 9).

The gentleness of Jesus had worked. The scribes and Pharisees arrived all fired-up ready to do battle and to trap Jesus into defending Moses' law so they could accuse Him, but they left one by one in total defeat and guilt.

The gentleness and goodness of our Lord continued. He stood up, looked around, and saw no one. Turning to the adulteress, He said, " 'Then neither do I condemn you,' Jesus declared. 'Go now and leave your life of sin' " (vv. 10–11).

What a gentle, compassionate Savior and Friend. What an example for us to put into practice! But be careful; gentleness is sometimes mistaken for watering-down the message, or flavoring the cod-liver oil. This is not what gentleness is all about. The method of application can be changed, but the unchanged message must always be applied boldly!

Christ also demonstrated meekness. When we've been cheated, we tend to want revenge. God said, "Vengeance is mine" (Rom. 12:19; Heb. 10:30; Ps. 94:1; Deut. 32:35). God doesn't just say that, leaving the new Christian sitting there frustrated, red in the face, and ready to get even. He shows us how to love our enemies and how to show goodness. Jesus said, "I tell you who hear me: Love your enemies, do good to those who hate you, [how?] bless those who curse you, pray for those who mistreat you. [example] If someone strikes you on one cheek, turn to him the other also. [another example] If someone takes your cloak, do not stop him from taking your tunic. [instructions] Give to everyone who asks you, and if anyone takes what belongs to you, do not demand it back. [In other words:] Do to others as you would have them do to you" (Luke 6:27–31). What an example and witness!

Can you honestly say that you are meek? I can't, but praise God I have a Savior who can. Jesus Christ is my complete substitute! Salvation, therefore, becomes the awareness that we cannot make it on our own. We must be salvaged and sustained by Christ Jesus.

Christ's Spirit also Contains Temperance

Temperance is that area of our personality where all the attributes of Christ's spirit are exercised in harmony. Jesus displayed temperance during His temptation. He practiced it in every mode of His life; yet there were those who still misunderstood and accused Him of all sorts of things. Jesus Himself said He was called "gluttonous" and a "winebibber," even a "drunkard." Did Jesus give offense, or did some take offense? There's an enormous difference.

How Does Our Temperance Compare with His?

Without temperance one often takes offense without offense being given. Unless temperance is personalized self-control—as opposed to the whims of everyone else in the community—it is an excercise in futility. Unless temperance arises out of one's own judgment, it is useless. Suppose you are at a sporting event of some kind, an exciting one. You attend with all your friends from church. The score is close; so you find yourself cheering until you lose your voice. The next Sunday in church with the same group of people, you would not dare so much as whisper an amen to a statement glorifying Christ because you feel you might be considered abnormal. What nonsense to be controlled by others. That's not temperance; that's surrender!

Temperance is not always the middle-of-the road approach either. One very obvious case would be the actual sin-plans of some who are misled by the devil enough to believe that they can go ahead and sin a little. That's not temperance; that's spiritual suicide!

Temperance is self-restraint in conduct. It may be indulgences, moderations, and even abstinences; but it is always Spirit led in every born-again Christian just as it was in our Lord.

Perhaps all that has been said so far about Christ's Spirit has pointed out a real need to substitute our weaknesses and faults for His perfection. We do this in faith. "For by grace are you saved through faith."

15

The Prayer Life of the New Christian

Jesus prayed! Your first reaction to that statement may be, "Of course He did. So what? Why is that so exciting?" Because He was the Son of God, equal to God, very God Himself; yet while on earth He felt the necessity, the real need, to pray to the Father. He is not only our Mediator in prayer but our example also.

Prayer is a *gift* because it represents a toll-free means of communication to our heavenly Father along "lines" which had the installation charges prepaid by our Mediator. Jesus said, "I am the way—and the truth and the life. No one comes to the Father except through me" (John 14:6). Prayer is futile without Jesus Christ!

We are told by Paul that "the Spirit helps us in our weakness. We do not know how we ought to pray, but the Spirit himself intercedes for us with groans that words cannot express" (Rom. 8:26). The Holy Spirit is not only the originator of every prayer but an integral part as well. We see here the interrelationship between us and the Trinity as well as the interrelationship between the three Persons of the Trinity. God's divinity interacts with our humanity. What a stunning realization this should be to the new convert and to all who seriously desire to envelop their efforts in prayer.

In this chapter, we will consider five truths concerning prayer: (1) not all our prayers are heard; (2) how to pray in the will of God; (3) a few conditions for answered prayer; (4) some reasons for possible delays in answered prayer; and (5) when we should quit praying. By looking at our own prayer life closely, we will better equip ourselves to counsel others.

Not All "Prayers" Are Heard

Many who do not receive an immediate answer to their prayer conclude that God has answered with a no. There's another possibility: Maybe God never heard the prayer in the first place.

Vain babblings, selfish requests, and self-centered desires are heard by God but not as prayer. Scripture refers several times to unheard prayers. Perhaps the clearest example is God's own statement: "And though they cry in mine ears with a loud voice, yet will I not hear them" (Ezek. 8:18, KJV)! In Proverbs, God said He will hide His face when we pray in our own will: "Then shall they call upon me, but I will not answer; they shall seek me early, but they shall not find me" (Prov. 1:28, KJV). In Isaiah God said, "When you spread out your hands in prayer, I will hide my eyes from you; even if you offer many prayers, I will not listen" (Isa. 1:15). Why? Here are some possible reasons.

God rewards them that diligently and earnestly seek Him (Heb. 11:6). Some of our prayers may not be heard because we refuse to seek God diligently.

We try to go it alone or get by with progress reports to

God. Jesus said, "But seek first his kingdom and his righteousness, and all these things will be given to you as well" (Matt. 6:33). What did Jesus mean? Unless we are diligently seeking Him, we are actually seeking ourselves; unless we are forsaking ourselves—losing our wills to His will in prayer—we are forsaking Him.

There are other rather specific reasons He does not always hear us. If we fail to humble ourselves, repent, and turn from our wicked ways (2 Chron. 7:11), He will not hear us. Also we must exercise the fruit of His Spirit in order to be heard. Patience, for example, surely was not exercised by the Israelites during the period of time when Moses was receiving the Ten Commandments. When Moses returned, he found that their lack of patience had brought them into even worse sins. Moses had to report that "the Lord was wroth with me for your sakes, and would not hear me" (Deut. 3:26, KJV). God also does not hear our prayers when our motive is wrong. When we are self-centered or pleasure seeking, God says, "When you ask, you do not receive, because you ask with wrong motives, that you may spend what you get on your pleasures" (James 4:3). Our Lord desires that we, as well as every new convert, understand the seriousness of prayer and realize the terrible price He had to pay to establish it. When a prayer is really for our own sakes, how dare we end it with "for Jesus' sake"? Such prayers are an abomination (Prov. 28:9).

God doesn't hear the proud either. Jesus taught us that "everyone who exalts himself will be humbled, and he who humbles himself will be exalted" (Luke 18:14). God won't hear those who offer empty babblings, for Jesus said, "They have received their reward in full" (Matt. 6:5). God won't listen to vain repetitions and traditional clichés when they are offered in place of prayer. Jesus reminds us, "And when you pray, do not keep on babbling like pagans, for they think they will be heard" (Matt. 6:7).

Maybe God doesn't hear our prayer because of our relationships at home. (Are you ready for this one?) God said, "Live with your wives, . . . treat them with respect . . . that nothing will hinder your prayers" (1 Pet. 3:7).

Our prayers will not be heard if we become discouraged and stop praying too soon. When we quit praying, we don't need an answer! Jesus said in Luke 18:1 that we "should always pray and not give up." Read Luke 18:1–8 to see what Jesus had to say about persistence in prayer. If it's really for Jesus' sake, faint not.

Our prayers will not be heard if we become too up-tight about problems and seek solutions of our own making, cutting God right out of it. God said, "In everything, by prayer and petition, with thanksgiving, present your requests to God" (Phil. 4:6).

Our prayers will not be heard if we are living a double standard. On the one hand we ask God to take specific notice of our activities, and on the other we exhibit behavior that we wouldn't even want our children (let alone God) to see. God said, "A double-minded man, [is] unstable in all he does. . . . That man should not think he will receive anything of the Lord" (James 1:8, 7, in that order).

It is quite obvious that the quip "His prayer never got any higher than the ceiling" is not so far out after all.

The Will of God in Our Prayer Lives

The primary reason our prayers are not heard can be summed up in one simple fact: We request things outside His will. All of the above could be classified under this one general fault. Christ taught us this lesson in His prayer on the Mount of Olives: "Father, if you are willing, take this cup from me; yet not my will, but yours be done" (Luke 22:42). Praying in accordance with His will may mean praying in deference to God's will as Jesus did. Taking ourselves out of the picture is the first step toward placing Christ first in our lives.

Submitting to God's will is not a psychological cop-out; it's common sense. Scripture plainly teaches this. His will comes to pass here upon earth (Matt. 6:10) despite our wishes; so doing His will might just as well be a full-time desire for us (John 4:34). The Bible also teaches that only one will exists anyway—the Father's (John 5:30). We must not only *do* His will, however, we must also understand why we are doing it. Paul said, "Do not be foolish, but understand what the Lord's will is" (Eph. 5:17).

A Few Conditions for Answered Prayer

One necessary ingredient to answered prayer is that the prayer must be in accord with God's will, not merely validate ours. The second vital ingredient is faith. "Faith is being sure of what we hope for and certain of what we do not see" (Heb. 11:1). Jesus demonstrated such faith when He prayed for Lazarus. Lazarus had been dead for four days and was stinking from decay (John 11:39). But before Jesus cried, "Lazarus, come out" (John 11:43), He demonstrated His faith in prayer—faith that he *would* come out—and thanked God for hearing this prayer. He *then* "called in a loud voice, 'Lazarus, come out!'" Lazarus was raised from the dead. Here faith is demonstrated by confident thanksgiving—in the same prayer request.

Another prerequisite to answered prayer is righteous living. The Psalmist said, "No good thing will he withhold from them that walk uprightly" (Ps. 84:11, KJV). But how many of us really walk uprightly every minute of every day?

Finally, to be answered, we must pray in the name of Jesus. In Him are found all the prerequisites for perfection required by God. This includes Christ's perfect worthiness for us and God's righteousness. Hallelujah, Jesus did it all, and He died praying for us! But Jesus was not a loner in His prayer life. He often invited His disciples to pray with Him. The Bible also gives other examples of group prayer: "They all joined together constantly in prayer, along with the women and Mary the mother of Jesus, and his brothers" (Acts 1:14), and in Acts 12:12 we read: "Many people had gathered and were praying."

The Bible also tells us to pray without ceasing. Have you ever wondered how this is accomplished? I used to be puzzled until I met some friends who could talk almost without breathing. After listening to them for awhile, I could better understand Paul's words: "We will give ourselves continually to prayer" (Acts 6:4, KJV).

Perhaps the most difficult biblical example of prayer to follow literally is the instruction to be thankful no matter what. "Do not be anxious about anything, but in everything, by prayer and petition, with thanksgiving, present your requests to God" (Phil. 4:6). This can be hard at times; yet it is a prerequisite to answered prayer.

Possible Delays in Answered Prayer

But what about those prayers which are offered by the Christian according to God's will that should have been heard and answered, but, so far, nothing? What happened?

Praying for something specific and not receiving it immediately is not necessarily a no answer or an unheard prayer. The Lord's timetable isn't ours. God once said, "My thoughts are not your thoughts, neither are your ways my ways" (Isa. 55:8, KJV); and in retrospect, we find that He's never late either.

There are times when we pray according to all the prerequisites of His will, and no answer comes. In His wisdom, God may be withholding the yes for a season or two—or even more. There are at least eight reasons why God might want us to wait for His answer.

1. God may want to teach us the patience of waiting.
2. God may want to increase our faith through waiting.
3. God may want us to become more earnest in our praying.
4. God may want to lead us into Scripture to learn the reason why.
5. God may want to prepare us for the yes answer.
6. God may want to test our faith.
7. God may want to give us a taste of affliction to better accept his peace.
8. God may be asking us to shape up first.

Praise God for the relief of answered prayer when it does come, for the patience to wait until it comes, and for the ability to recognize His love even if it never comes or comes differently from the way we "ordered" it.

When to Pray and When to Quit Praying

Persistence stands out as a quality of Jesus' prayer life. His prayers could be studied and studied until, it seems to me, we would almost not dare to pray for fear of doing it wrongly. This feeling may be particularly strong in the new convert, but we must always bear in mind that God loves believers and wants to talk with His own through His Word and through our prayers.

Perhaps the most important time to pray is when we feel least like it. God already knows our hearts and has rectified the "whole of our prayer" as well as the "holes in our prayers." Jesus doesn't want us frustrated in prayer; so He says, "Your Father knows what you need before you ask him" (Matt. 6:8). Praise God for our Lord's perceptivity and His love for us. He really cares!

Probably the best advice we ever received from God on beginning a prayer is hidden in one of those psalms we had to commit to memory as children. "Enter . . . with thanksgiving, and . . . praise; be thankful unto him, and bless his name" (Ps. 100:4, kjv). The text talks about worshiping Him in His courts; and what is prayer if it's not worshiping Him in thanksgiving? The primary purpose of all prayer is thanksgiving.

Once we've begun to pray the right way, our spirits will be in harmony with God's Spirit. Then we will allow God's Spirit to take over our thoughts and our requests, perfecting them (modifying them if necessary) while we pray. When we find ourselves in submission to His will our prayers will be heard and answered.

When do we quit praying? When do we stop asking God for something? There are many answers to that question, but we should be alert to God's prompting us to cease our requests for something He chooses not to give us. When that "something" becomes an obsession, we sin. When that "something" becomes impossible to obtain because God has shut all the doors, we should quit praying. When we submit, prayer becomes Christ's sincere desire instead of ours. God instructs us to align our priorities to coincide with His will. Thank God for His perfect will!

16

Jesus Then and Now

In this chapter we will look at Jesus from a different point of view in order to acquaint the new and the mature Christian with facts that influenced our Lord's life, humanly speaking, while He walked among us—His birth, His childhood, and His public ministry. We will also look at His physical world, His political world, His intellectual world, His religious world, and His moral and social world in an effort, not only to know Him better, but to reflect Him as a relevant, understanding, reliable, pertinent Savior with today's perspectives and solution in hand. Often we'll be forced into demonstrating how Jesus can possibly be relevant to our day. Did He ever work an assembly line, endure old age, raise rebellious teenagers? This chapter confronts that larger problem of how much Jesus lived as a creature of His time and place and whether He applies to ours.

Some Factors That Influenced Our Lord's Life

Jesus Christ was authentic. He became disgusted and showed it, He became depressed and wept, and He became physically "beat." He had a good sense of humor, and He relates to us today in such a way that twentieth-century humankind can, and may, identify with Him.

In His outward appearance, which psychologists claim manifests an inner ego, Jesus appeared quite normal. Probably He was not an overly handsome man. The Bible says of Him: "He grew up before him like a tender shoot, and like a root out of dry ground. He had no beauty or majesty to attract us to him, nothing in his appearance that we should desire him" (Isa. 53:2). But his appearance did not take on the opposite extreme either (Ps. 45:2). He probably dressed well since the Roman soldiers cast lots for His seamless garment rather than cut it up.

He may have *looked* older than He really was. The final conclusion to that probability is left to you after you check John 8:57 where the Jews said of Jesus, "You are not yet fifty years old."

It is very doubtful that He wore a beard or long hair as the artists picture Him because such was not the custom with the Jews of that day. Furthermore, Paul stated that it was a dishonor for a man to wear his hair long (1 Cor. 11:14). Would Paul, who was one to be all things to all men, make such a statement as this if Jesus, his Master, wore His hair long?

When we say that Jesus was just like us in all things except sin, we often forget that Jesus not only knew the purpose for which He came into the world (just as we do) but that He also knew (we don't) exactly how He would accomplish it. This factor had to play an important role in the development of Christ's personality, in the human sense. Whereas we must spend a lifetime searching out God's will for our lives, Christ could have read and memorized God's will for His life in Isaiah 53.

Rejection started before birth: "No room . . . in the inn." It followed Him to the cross where He was crucified, rejected, and despised. He is still rejected today, every day.

His Birth

Jesus was born in the year 4 or 5 B.C. (before Christ). This is a mathematical quirk of man, not of God. He came to earth as the Son of God (Matt. 3:17), having been born of a virgin (Luke 1:27). He lived an obedient life (Rom. 5:19), and He did not sin (1 Pet. 2:22). He remained humble throughout his life (Phil. 2:5–11). He lived in poverty as contrasted to the glory one might attribute to Him (2 Cor. 8:9). The Good News is that He did this for us (John 3:16–17).

Psychologists maintain that the events of early life, including prenatal existence, are basic to everyone's personality traits. In this regard, Jesus probably suffered from the trauma of a young mother's anxiety (walking about visibly pregnant and unwed), from the physical abuse that no doubt occurred during the long journey into Bethlehem just prior to His birth, and from the pressures Mary experienced in finding a suitable place to deliver her child.

Mary and Joseph searched, but there was "no room"; so God became incarnate in a manger. The no-room aspect has not changed in our changing world. Christ is still crowded out of politics, business, pleasure, literature, and now even out of the laws of our land. He is crowded out of some churches and families with the same excuse used then: no room . . . here.

Infancy to Twelve

We know that as a baby He was cuddled. Simeon was one who held the infant Jesus (Luke 2:28). He was admired by even more (Matt. 2). Before two years of age, He was whisked off into Africa to avoid King Herod (Matt. 2:13–15). He lived in Egypt before being taken back to Nazareth where the whole trip to Bethlehem had originated. At the age of two, Jesus was in Nazareth for the first time.

Jesus and John the Baptist were only six months apart in age, and it is conceivable (though there is no record of it) that Mary and Joseph may have stopped by to see Elisabeth and Zacharias (parents of John the Baptist) since they passed only a few miles from their home enroute back to Nazareth. *If* Jesus and John ever played together as children (remember that Mary and Elisabeth were related), their relationship would have been a very normal one. We read that John the Baptist did not know who Jesus really was until about six months prior to the beginning of Christ's ministry.

During the later years of Christ's childhood, He had to learn give-and-take in a household of younger children. Have you ever wondered if the sinless Jesus ever "bugged" the other children?

In the Temple at the age of twelve, He confounded the wise men with His understanding and wisdom. We can assume from this glimpse of our Lord that He knew of His divine mission and His divine nature at this point, that He was a very good student of the Scriptures, and that He was obedient to His parents. We hear nothing about Him for the next eighteen years!

The Eighteen Years of Silence

About the only thing we can say about those silent years is that our Lord probably lost His earthly father; Joseph is not mentioned again after the Temple incident. This would mean, of course, that whatever effect such a loss would have had on Jesus He began His earthly ministry without Joseph having lived to witness it.

His Public Ministry

His public ministry began as devoid of public display as His birth. At the initiation of His ministry, He just appeared! From over a hill, He came walking down to the river bank to John the Baptist and a baptismal ceremony. Remember, John didn't know who Jesus was until six months prior to this event. John marvels at this himself: "I myself did not know him" (John 1:31). "I would not have known him, except that the one who sent me to baptize with water told me" (John 1:33). However, when Jesus walked over the hill, John knew! He said, "Look, the Lamb of God, who takes away the sin of the world" (John 1:29). John's total ministry only lasted eighteen months before he was beheaded. All that time, John was "decreasing" himself so that Christ would "increase." John, therefore, accomplished in eighteen months what many of us scarcely try in our lifetime, namely, the reduction of our own ego and personality in the advancement of Christ's.

Jesus was baptized on the first day of His public ministry. He was sinless; yet at that time baptism was the symbol of moral cleansing (Luke 3:14) and represented repentance (Matt. 3:11). Today baptism is a sacrament, instituted by

Christ Himself as a sign and seal of the covenant. Why did Jesus desire to be baptized? Obviously this was not a Christian baptism. Jesus was sinless. He needed no pardon. He did *not* do it as a substitution for us—a fact demonstrated by the later institution of the sacrament. By this act, however, He identified Himself with those He came to save, pointing up the difference between receiving pardon, the symbol of baptism then, and bestowing pardon, the purpose of His very life.

During the first exchanges of words between our Lord and John the Baptist, we see a division of opinion. This came from the same lack of understanding with which Jesus would have to contend throughout all His earthly ministry. The task of having to set the record straight time after time had to affect Christ. He knew this would be the case: "Do you think I came to bring peace on earth? No, I tell you, but division" (Luke 12:51). John described this divided opinion concerning His public ministry in these words: "Among the crowds there was widespread whispering about him. Some said, 'He is a good man.' Others replied, 'No, he deceives the people'" (John 7:12). "Thus the people were divided because of Jesus" (John 7:43; see also John 9:16, 10:19).

This division led to total rejection. The people of Nazareth rejected Him (Mark 6:3; Luke 4:28–29). The chief priests and rulers rejected Him (Luke 23:18), and the whole Jewish nation rejected Him: "He came unto his own, and his own received him not" (John 1:11, KJV). The business of disdaining Christ did not end at the cross or at the ascension. Nor has it yet today!

Jesus' Physical World

Jesus grew up in Nazareth in what is today Israel. The land area is about as little as New Hampshire, but the Bible called it "a land flowing with milk and honey" (Exod. 3:8, KJV). It's located in a semitropical climate with summers tempered by the cool mountain air and winters shortened because of its southern geographical location. This same piece of real estate was called Canaan before the Israelites inhabited the land (Gen. 16:3, 17:8), and Israel after that. Then the southern part was called Judea following the captivity (Mark 1:5), and the whole land Palestine since the days of Christ.

For the most part, transportation facilities were confined to foot. We should bear in mind this slower pace when considering the journeys our Lord took. Horse-drawn chariots existed as well as boats, but they didn't move much faster. Journeys were measured by "Sabbath day's journey," whereas we measure journeys by how long it takes to jet there. A flight from New York to Tel Aviv takes about twelve hours today.

Jesus' Political World

Politics is probably almost as old as Adam and Eve. Certainly the citizens of Jesus' day found it no less important than we do. Because of a politician's lack of character, Jesus was finally turned over to the crowd to be crucified. Politics cost John the Baptist his head; James, his life; and Paul and Peter, jail terms (Acts 12).

The politicians of the Roman Senate had appointed Herod the Great as the first foreigner to rule directly over the Jews in Palestine. After Herod's death, the "precincts" were divided (because of Herod's last will and testament) among three of his sons as though the ability to rule might be transferred by heredity alone.

Archelaus received Judea and Samaria (Matt. 2). Galilee and Perea were given to Antipas, whom Jesus later called a fox (Luke 13:32). Philip received and ruled over Iturea. The latter two tetrarchs, as they were designated, remained in office all through Christ's life on earth; but Archelaus, the tetrarch of Judea and Samaria, was impeached by Augustus in A.D. 6 for being excessively cruel to the Jews.

We can safely assume, on the basis that Jesus lived a normal childhood, that political events such as these would have aroused a natural curiosity in His mind. His world was yet untainted by a full human knowledge of hatred and violence. At any rate, various Roman procurators held the office of tetrarch until 26 when Pontius Pilate took over. Pontius Pilate was in office from 26 until 36, which included the time of Christ's crucifixion. Pilate's name is remembered even today as we recite the Apostles' Creed and call to mind that our Lord suffered under Pontius Pilate, who was obviously influenced more by politics than by Christ. Pilate consistently avoided responsibility by turning Jesus over to the Jewish authorities (John 18:31), by sending Him to Herod (Luke 23:7), by proposing a minor penalty (Luke 23:22), by diverting the attention to Barabbas (Matt. 27:17), and by the use of a hypocritical ceremony (Matt. 27:24). He was not the last person or government to make these mistakes. Often we tend to pass the buck, especially in areas of our own moral irresponsibility.

Jesus' Intellectual World

The intellectual world in which Jesus grew up was quite advanced and highly developed. This advancement, however, was not as great in everyday Jewish culture as in Greco-Roman culture. Language, literature, art, philosophy, and science were highly developed among the Greeks. While God used the Jews as His instrument to bring salvation to the earth in the Person of His Son Jesus Christ, He mobilized Greco-Roman culture as the matrix *into* which He could place Christianity and have it develop into a universal world religion.

Jesus' Religious World

Christ was destined to overturn the "religious" world into which He came. Many of His fellow Jews were intensely religious—fanatical, self-righteous, and legalistic. They were known for their practice of religion, but much of it did not please Jesus. He came to replace their laws with Himself.

The people of Jesus' time knew about the "Messianic prophecies," but they had two applications for them. In the narrow sense, they referred to all the specific predictions of a unique personality, the Messiah. In the broader sense, they included all the great institutions of the Hebrew nation—the prophetic order, the monarchy, and the priesthood.

The development of the Messianic predictions was plainly delineated by God in Scripture, but the Jews managed somehow to forget or overlook much of it in their broadening concept of the Messianic hope. God stated in the Old Testament that the Messiah would be a descendant of Abraham (Gen. 12:3), from the tribe of Judah (Gen. 49:10), and from the house of David (Isa. 11:1). He would be the Messenger of the covenant (Mal. 3:1), a Prophet sent by God (Deut. 18:15, 18, fulfilled in Acts 3:22), a Priest (Ps. 110:4, revealed in Heb. 5:6), and King (Zech. 9:9, evidenced in Matt. 21:5). But the Jews of Jesus' day did not recognize Him because they expected a political figure, one who would seek revenge on all oppressors and create for them an earthly empire.

There were three religious sects among the Jews of Jesus' day, two of them important to us here. First, the Pharisees, the "conservative formalists." They were separatists, distinguished from other Jews by their "superior" holiness. (Nicodemus and Paul were of this sect at one time.) The Pharisees rejected Christ because of His humble origin and lack of higher education (Matt. 13:55–57), because of the "bad" company He kept (Luke 15:2), and because He opposed their ceremonialism and their ideas on keeping the Sabbath.

Jesus, on the other hand, opposed the Pharisees because of their misunderstanding of who the Messiah really was, their narrow-minded formality, and their self-righteousness. These are a few of the problems we all share today. Jesus is relevant to us!

Second, there were the Sadducees, the "intellectuals." Because they denied many of the Pharisaical beliefs, there was dissension between the two groups. The Sadducees did not feel obligated to obey the elaborate teachings of the Pharisees, nor did they believe in the resurrection. In fact, they denied it (Matt. 22:23). The Sadducees also denied the existence of angels or spirits (Acts 5:12–19). Politically, they were close to the Romans.

Jesus' Moral and Social World

The moral and social world in which our Lord found Himself was wicked, wealthy at the top, and decayed. Moral degradation was not worse than it has ever been, but the first century A.D. wasn't the Garden of Eden either! Paul described it in these words: "Although they claimed to be wise, they became fools and exchanged the glory of the immortal God for images made to look like mortal man and birds and animals and reptiles" (Rom. 1:22–23). With the advent of voodoo, other forms of witchcraft, and X-rated movies, are we seeing the same situation repeat itself? Paul went on to say, "Therefore God gave them over in the sinful desires of their hearts to sexual impurity for the degrading of their bodies with one another" (Rom. 1:24). Perhaps Paul's next words most accurately describe what happened in the Garden of Eden: "They exchanged the truth of God for a lie, and worshiped and served created things rather than the Creator—who is forever praised" (Rom. 1:25). Is our situation any different from that described in Romans 1:22–25? Sin was, is, and will continue to be the single force that drives us from God. It was no different in Jesus' day.

17

The Secret Is Balance

In a way, it's a shame to frame this chapter as the last when all of life depends so heavily on balance; yet it's only at this point that we can best understand and assimilate the concept.

God said a few things about balance. A significant comment, for example, occurs in Ecclesiastes 3:1–8: "To every thing there is a season, and a time to every purpose under the heaven: A time to be born, and a time to die; a time to plant, and a time to pluck up that which is planted; A time to kill, and a time to heal; a time to break down, and a time to build up; A time to weep, and a time to laugh; a time to mourn, and a time to dance; A time to cast away stones, and a time to gather stones together; a time to embrace, and a time to refrain from embracing; A time to get, and a time to lose; a time to keep, and a time to cast away; A time to rend, and a time to sew; a time to keep silence, and a time to speak; A time to love, and a time to hate; a time of war, and a time of peace" (KJV). This passage strikes me as one where God, once again, stoops down to our level of understanding and our frame of reference, since God Himself is timeless.

The factor of balance as related to Jesus has been mentioned often throughout this book; yet there is so much more to our Lord's balance which applies to witnessing.

God, in Christ, is extremely merciful; but God—in balance —is also authoritatively just. No one outside Christ can escape His just judgment and punishment. Jesus Christ is our clearest evidence of God's love. The balancing side, however, is God's justice and eternal damnation for those who haven't reordered their lives in that perfect substitutionary life of Christ. The free gift of salvation in Jesus Christ must be balanced by an active and responsible discipleship of good works, for faith without works is dead.

Balance exists everywhere. It is the theme of God's special revelation as given in Holy Scripture as well as the theme of God's general revelation in nature. Jesus Christ, the Word become flesh, represents that perfect balance between both revelations.

Balance surrounds our Christian life. Every crisis contains the grace to survive it. Through Christ's bankruptcy, we gain eternal wealth; with the death of our old self comes eternal life; with Jesus' agony came His joy on the cross and our joy. With questions directed toward God in the Name of Jesus come answers of survival. Out of tribulation comes Jesus' peace.

Each effect has a cause, and every cause produces an effect. Frustration generates action, and the forerunner of understanding is often confusion. God's wrath demands our death, but God's love through Jesus Christ guarantees our eternal life in a reorganized balance reconstructed by God.

Some causes and effects, however, must be balanced by us! For instance, zeal must be balanced with patience. Paul said he was "all things to all men so that by all possible means I might save some" (1 Cor. 9:22), but he also said, "Let your gentleness [moderation] be evident to all" (Phil.

4:5). Prayer has to be balanced by action; in fact we often become humorous to God in this area. When we pray, pray, pray, never getting up off our knees to receive the answer, we are only doing half of God's requirement. In business matters also, the Bible shows us a balance. On the one hand, we are told to cast all our cares upon Him. This is the prayer part of the balance. The action part comes from another text: "Be . . . not slothful in business." James' familiar words depict both prayer and action—in balance: "Be ye doers of the word, and not hearers only" (James 1:22, KJV).

There is more to this life of equilibrium. Some areas we tend to overbalance, as when we compare our personalities with the personality of Jesus Christ. He radiates forgiveness, and we tend to seek revenge; He forgets when He forgives, we tend to remember and throw it back later. Jesus gives freely; we tend to loan, demanding security. Jesus was friendly to all men; we choose our friends instead and thumb our righteous noses at the less blessed. Our Lord's personality was exalted through His humiliation: we try to gain through self-exaltation and then fall right on our faces.

Some proportions never change because the entire matter is in His control: the balance between total depravity and complete forgiveness, the balance between reprobation and election, and the balance between human responsibility and God's sovereignty.

Balance is also the central thought behind all of God's Word. His symmetry must be allowed to influence ours: God's Word tells us that when we live an imbalanced life we are carnal.

Carnal Christians

Carnal Christians, though saved (Paul calls them brothers), are confused, frustrated, and often defeated by Satan. To their own disgust, they tend to destroy their witness. Carnal Christians know and experience two kinds of life: the world's and the Christian's. They are in a constant battle with good and evil while inwardly at conflict with their own souls. They are the very reason non-Christians call them hypocrites. They are frustrated, full of impure thoughts; yet they are Christians. They continue to sin and rationalize their sin rather than constantly seek forgiveness. They doubt when they are not in (studying) God's Word. They have an "off-again, on-again" prayer life; yet these are born-again Christians. Paul said, "I could not address you as spiritual but as worldly [carnal]—mere infants in Christ" (1 Cor. 3:1).

God Wants to Know from the Carnal Christian . . .

When will you learn that there is no other way? That you are nothing apart from Me? That I'm right about everything I've ever told you or warned you? That you are hopelessly incapable of performing a single act of goodness or obedience apart from Me? That you are foredefeated in fighting the devil alone? That the skills which enhance your reputation are merely My gifts to you? That the next breath of air isn't yours to inhale unless I give it to you? That while you were still hopelessly lost and sinning, I gave you Jesus, My Son? When will you learn to know Me so that boasting in yourselves will be as pointless to you as it is to Me? When will you learn that your salvation didn't stop at Calvary but

goes beyond the cross into today? That for each new genera-
tion there is a whole new world to be conquered for Me?
That I have entrusted my eternal truth to you so that you
can go and tell someone?

Natural Man

The balanced Word of God tells us there are three kinds
of people: the non-Christian, the carnal Christian, and the
spiritual Christian. The non-Christian is called the natural
man; and the Bible says of him: "The natural man receiveth
not the things of the Spirit of God: for they are foolishness
unto him: neither can he know them, because they are spiritually discerned" (1 Cor. 2:14, KJV).

Spiritual Christians

The Spiritual man is Christ-controlled and fruitful. He is
pleasing to those with whom he comes into contact, not ir-
ritating or sour. In fact, he is a reflection of love, joy, peace,
long-suffering, gentleness, goodness, faith, meekness, and
temperance.

But even the most spiritual person alive is nothing much
without Christ rebalancing him. He is only spiritual because
Christ has balanced his total life.

The best way to illustrate this is to use an example, one I
heard my pastor apply so well from the pulpit. A family had
arrived at a resort area high in the mountains and were staying at a small hotel. In the lobby of the hotel was an old
piano. The youngest daughter of the family had recently

begun taking piano lessons, just enough of them to know how to pick out a tune with one finger. She would go over to the piano daily and sit there finger-picking at the same tune, hitting many sour notes in the process. This finally began to irritate others sitting in the lobby.

One day a world famous pianist arrived at the hotel, and overheard the little girl playing the piano. He went over to her and asked if he could sit down next to her on the bench. Soon he began to play along with her simple tune a series of soft backup chords, one for every note she played, even those off-key.

The little girl's music no longer irritated those in the lobby, and soon many of the hotel guests were gathering at the piano to listen. Each note, plunked out with but one finger, was backed up with full harmonious chords, each combined in a proportionate and orderly arrangement which gave the total sound an acceptable, pleasing, and appealing affect. When the little girl was finished playing, the famous musician said to everyone gathered: "Doesn't she do well?"

The point of this illustration is this: Even the most lovable person alive must admit that if he were only half of what some think him to be, he'd be twice what he really is, because Christ is the filler, even in the most spiritual person. If we give God our best efforts in witnessing, He will "fill in" with the witness of His Spirit, balancing it all into a beautiful victory in Christ—but we must plunk out one witness at a time, just as the little girl hit one note at a time (even a few off-key) while Christ embodies it into an appealing success for His Kingdom.

Just as the little girl's music needed fillers to be appreciated, so the Christian's life needs the Master to balance it, thus making it beautiful to God, while appealing to His own here on earth. The "harmony" needed is Jesus. He is the Word become flesh. The balance contained in God's Word is Jesus, the filler in every witness for Him.

Our Challenge

On the authority of God's Word, join me in a systematic program of Bible study (regardless of how mature you may be) in order to mature in the faith. Go out and win souls for Christ, but grow *with* each new convert.

Praise to You, Jesus, for being God and man; for ingrafting Your balanced and perfect personality into our personalities and still allowing us to be uniquely ourselves; for being our Friend; for giving us the free gift of eternal life in and with You; for being victorious, not only over death but over life too; for giving us Your Holy Spirit; and for entrusting us to present, magnify, and reflect that balanced picture of who You are—God's rainbow in the mud puddles of our lives. Yes, thank You, Jesus!

Now we must go out, every one of us, and reflect the Person of Jesus Christ who dwells within through His Spirit. Quoting the Old Testament Paul stated that some of our contacts will have these marks:

"Their throats are open graves;
    their tongues practice deceit."
"The poison of vipers is on their lips."
    "Their mouths are full of cursing and bitterness."
"Their feet are swift to shed blood;
    ruin and misery mark their paths,
and the way of peace they do not know."
    "There is no fear of God before their eyes."

Rom. 3:13–18

Praise God that He allows our throats to be open testimonies (instead of open graves); our tongues to sing His praises (instead of practice deceit); our lips to speak of life eternal (instead of viper's poison); our mouths to be full of thanksgiving (instead of cursing and bitterness); and our way—His way—the way of perfect peace we can only receive from Him. Praise God for eternity, but start right now!